FINDING FAMILY

STORIES OF CONNECTION AND HOPE

DON ECKERLE   STEPHEN D. EDWARDS   JOAN FOOR

CHRISTINA HOAG   DIANE KANE   MICHAEL P. KUSEN

DAVID LANGE   AMANDA MONTONI   H. NEWNAM

WILLIAM JOHN ROSTRON   JANET MAIKA'I RUDOLPH

RENÉE TONE   JASMINE TRITTEN   JANET METZ WALTER

The RedPenguin
COLLECTION

Finding Family–Stories of Connection and Hope

Copyright © 2022 by JK Larkin

Published by Red Penguin Books

Bellerose Village, New York

Library of Congress Control Number: 2022905573

ISBN

Print 978-1-63777-366-6

Digital 978-1-63777-367-3

CONTENTS

CUZ

DAVID LANGE

Our days are filled with colorful events and meaningful people. Like the pieces of a jigsaw puzzle, these come together to form a whole—the story of our lives. Sometimes, pieces of the puzzle are taken from us while other times they are misplaced and we long for their recovery. If you've ever gazed upon a nearly finished puzzle yet lack the remaining pieces to complete it, you'll understand the disquieting feeling that lingers and you'll understand the need to seek a remedy.

Broken Arm Summer. That's what I call it. It was the summer of 1972 and I was involved in an unfortunate misadventure at my local day camp, hosted at my elementary school. My sixth birthday was still a month or so away when, for the closing event of the day, our camp counselor elected to launch a bunch of wild Kindergarten grads into an uncontrolled game of "Brownies and Fairies." It was the one and only time in my life that I played "Brownies and Fairies." I had never heard of the game and I recall not being particularly enthusiastic when it was proposed to us. I am 99% certain that the counselor had no intention for this end-of-day diversion to turn into a violent free-for-all of tackling and high-speed bodily impacts. We were five and six so, of course, it did. Sure enough, I got tackled, the offending youth landing squarely on top of me as my left arm folded underneath my collapsing body. Nearly immediately, a horrible pain shot through my arm. The severity of the incident must have been apparent to the camp counselor as the game was stopped and I was escorted to the nurse's office. On the way, we stopped at a water fountain so I could rehydrate. I knew it was a bad thing when I found myself unable to bend over to reach the stream of water. My left shoulder was numb and, for reasons I can't explain, felt like it was sitting several inches above my right shoulder. It wasn't...but that's what it felt like. My father was called to come retrieve me as the nurse completed her inspection. "Will a piece of bubble gum make it feel better?" Those were the nurse's exact words. I remember them 50 years later because they made me incredibly angry. I didn't know many curse words back then but, if I did, I might well have cut loose with a stream of expletives. "No. Bubble gum won't make me feel better." I hated Brownies and Fairies and I hated day camp and I was in the most extreme pain of my young life. I'm sure my angry glare and abrupt response made my point effectively.

Eventually, my father showed up. My Mom was out with the car and, in the pre-cell phone days, there was no way to contact her. We were going to have to walk home. I was barely out of the school building when I realized that I wasn't going to be able to make it. The initial adrenalin rush and numbness were subsiding and now I was feeling intense, teeth-grinding pain with each step I took. I made it to the edge of the school property when the situation became untenable. In an act of gallantry that I remember still, to this day, my father decided he was going to carry me home. I must have weighed somewhere between 45 and 50 pounds yet my father completed the half mile walk, much of it uphill, while carrying his injured and wriggling son. I felt very proud of my dad.

When Mom returned with the vehicle, I was taken to the doctor's office and our fears were confirmed—broken arm. My arm was bandaged, splinted and secured firmly against the side of my body with some very aggressive wrapping. It was awful. That was the end of my summer...or so I thought. I was in for a wonderful surprise, one that would redeem what I thought was a lost summer vacation.

Family. I've always been somewhat envious of those large families with innumerable grandparents, aunts, uncles, and cousins living within close proximity. That was not my family. My father was an only child. My mother had one sister. My paternal grandmother had passed before my birth and, seeing as how they lived more than a day's drive away, we rarely saw my surviving grandparents, the last of whom passed away in 1992. In total, I can count the number of grandparent visits on two hands. I regret not knowing my grandparents better but I accepted it as part of life in a modern and mobile society. For all that, I still felt the absence of an extended family.

There was one and only one highlight during the summer of 1972—my maternal grandmother was coming to visit, along with my Aunt Carol and Cousin Sherril (Sheri). We sometimes referred to my grandmother as "Rootin' Tootin' Thelma." She was a wild one but lots of fun. It's quite possible that I met Grandma Thelma before this but, alas, any such memory is lost to me. I certainly had no memory of ever meeting my aunt or cousin before. It was a memorable day!

While the adults did their thing, my brother, sister, and I had a wonderful time playing with Cousin Sheri. She was fantastic and we immediately bonded. My brother is ten years older than me (twelve years older than my sister) so we enlisted the aid of Cousin Sheri to help us conspire against him in various plots. Several years older than my sister and I, Sheri made the perfect ally and was a willing conspirator in our fun games and older brother harassment schemes. It was an absolute blast! I just remember having so much fun and feeling so happy to have found not only a new family member, but also a friend. We all loved Sheri a lot and we were sad when she had to leave.

Years passed, and there was no reunion. In the fall of 1979, Grandma Thelma came to visit us in New York. We took her to the circus at Madison Square Garden and then to see *Annie* on Broadway. I was older and more mature than during Grandma's previous visit and I felt that we really bonded. I've always had a bit of a mischievous side and I know Grandma did, as well. I think she saw that spark in me and I in her. Sadly, it was the last time I would see my grandmother before she passed. All my grandparents were gone. My mother got to travel with her mom before we lost her, in 1992, and I'm glad she did. I regret not having profited from more time with all of my grandparents. I never felt like I really got to know them and what they knew of me was only as a young child. With the exception of a few visits to see my Great Aunt in South Dakota, who lived to be 102, I had no more contact with any extended family.

In 1984, I joined the Air Force and traveled the world. It was tough enough to make it back home to see my own parents let alone begin a search for extended family. I got married in 1993 and children followed several years later, four of them, to be specific. With few exceptions, I stopped going "home" for vacations since my new home was wherever my children were and that home traveled from state to state and country to country. Occasionally, my siblings and I would reminisce about that one special day when Cousin Sheri visited us. While obviously cognizant of the fact that Grandma and Aunt Carol were part of that visit, we ultimately focused on Sheri—she was one of us—a peer from our own generation. With the passing of time, the visit transformed from family reunion into something more resembling an urban legend. Did it really happen?

As the years passed, following the summer of '72, we would, upon occasion, receive photos in the mail and we'd race to see the photos of our cousin. It became more difficult to equate the images of a blossoming young woman with the mischievous kid who was our buddy and co-conspirator in the early 70s. Sheri was growing up. We all were. Yet, locked in our mind was the mental picture of our forever 9-year-old cousin. I often wondered what she was like now. I wondered if she remembered the fun we had in 1972 as fondly as we did. We revered the day. Time often widens the divide between people and, especially after my grandmother passed away, it seemed like we lost track of our cousin. While I've never heard my mother say a negative word about her sister, or vice versa, the fact remained that the two seldom communicated. I never heard them talk on the phone and, so far as I knew, they did little to communicate through other means, either. My aunt lived in Ohio. We lived in New York. That's just the way things were. I never stopped wondering about my cousin nor hoping that life was treating her well. Honestly, I didn't know. I was always a little bit uneasy about asking my parents about extended family. I don't exactly know why. I guess I figured that if they cared to share things with us then they would do so. The result was a patchwork of disconnected vignettes that created a confusing puzzle with numerous missing pieces. It bothered me...but I let it go.

Conceivably, things might have continued as they were. I'm glad they didn't. As it turns out, I really needed my cousin back in my life to help me through the challenges of the coming years. My marriage was slowly coming apart at the seams and my children, now mostly teens, no longer seemed interested in hanging out with their father. The years following 2010 seemed very lonely and I felt increasingly isolated, even in my own family. Work was tough and getting tougher and my projected military retirement was looming, menacingly, on the horizon. My life was about to enter the turbulent white water.

While visiting my parents for a few days of leave in the spring of 2014, my mom mentioned that Sherril had sent along a few old photos that I might be interested in seeing. Sherril had recently had to place her mother in a nursing home and she found some old photos of my mother that she thought would be nice to send our way. Old photos? Of course, I love old family photos. And then, like a bolt from the blue, it struck me. "Wait. Cousin Sherril sent photos? Through the mail???" Immediately, my mind made the connection that there was bound to be a return address on the package. Previously, I had no idea what my cousin's last name was. I was pretty sure she had gotten married but that's about all I knew. Without wasting a moment, I raced over to the package and copied the name. I felt incredibly inspired and, seconds later, I was searching social media. The prospect of possibly reconnecting with my lost cousin was incredibly exciting. I think my parents were startled by my enthusiasm and single-minded focus. My rapid tapping upon the screen of my cell phone must have appeared as some tribal sorcery to my parents who had never sent a text message nor used a smartphone in their lives. And then, Bingo! There she was. It had to be Cousin Sheri. I sent a Facebook friend request along with a message and I waited...and hoped. June 1, 2014—this was a very happy day...the day my beloved cousin and I reconnected. With introductions complete, I sent on a few old photos and then typed out a lengthy message about my life journey across the past 42 years since we had last seen each other. Shortly thereafter, Sherril reciprocated. As it turns out, we had both been longing for family and regretting that our childhoods were not filled with more familial connections. I could not have been happier to be reconnected with my cousin!

Not so very long after returning to my family in Louisiana, I received orders for a two-year assignment in South Korea. It was a stressful time and the assignment would, eventually, prove to be the final straw that broke the camel's back in my marriage. It was a very sad time in my life. The single saddest day of my life was the day I drove my family to the bus station on our base, in Seoul, South Korea, and hugged them goodbye. My soon-to-be ex-wife was returning to her hometown in South Dakota and she was taking my kids with her. I never felt so alone in all my life. Beyond having the support of my family back in New York, it proved to be an incredible blessing to have my cousin back in my life, too. I was hurting and I can't imagine how things would have gone were it not for my family's support.

On a brighter note, even though I was living in Korea, I thought it would be great to visit with my cousin and her family in Michigan. When work took me back to U.S. Transportation Command Headquarters, at Scott Air Force Base in Illinois, for a multi-week planning conference, I saw an opportunity to capitalize on the free weekend. This was my chance to finally reunite with my cousin after 44 years and get to meet her family. I was thrilled!

On Friday, May 13, 2016, I caught an evening flight up to Detroit and was met by Sherril's husband, Ken, at the airport. I could tell right away that he was a great guy. Sherril and Ken even put me up in a great hotel nearby. The next few days were filled with tons of fun. On Saturday, I got to see my cousin's son, Zach, working the course at a nearby skateboard park and then I got to assist with his little league practice. Later that day, despite the extremely frigid temperatures, we all went to a local fair after having a great lunch at a Middle Eastern restaurant. While visiting with my cousin and her family, I also had the opportunity to speak to my Aunt Carol on the phone. It was a great call and the first time I remember actually speaking with my aunt. The next day was equally as enjoyable as we all went to visit the Henry Ford Museum and Greenfield Village. I'd always wanted to visit the museum and it was wonderful to be able to see it with family. After the museum visit, we had a quick lunch together before I had to head to the airport to make my way back to Illinois to complete my work at the conference. It was tough to say goodbye.

In 2018, I finally retired from the Air Force, after a career that spanned more than 30 years. While I won't deny a deep hurt inside that my own children did not attend my retirement ceremony, I was eternally grateful that Sherril and her family drove all the way down (to Illinois) from Michigan to attend the event. I can't begin to tell you how special that was for me. Beyond this, my father, mother, sister, and nieces were able to attend. Since Mom, Dad, and my sister, Jennifer, had been present for my initial commissioning into the U.S. Air Force and graduation from the United States Air Force Academy, there seemed to be a beautiful symmetry to having them there for my final salute as an Air Force officer.

There's something special about family. Friends are great and, in many instances, may be as close, or closer than our own family. But, in my opinion, there's a timeless bond between family members sharing blood and ancestry. There's also a sacred trust. I feel stronger around family and I feel more at peace when family is near. For years, I stared at an incomplete puzzle, feeling unsatisfied. One of the greatest blessings of my life was returning an important piece to that picture as I found my wonderful cousin and, once again, we shared the love that comes from being united as family.

SEARCHING FOR MY LONG AGO
PAST IN LAGOS
CHRISTINA HOAG

"Don't get out of the car," the driver instructs as he winds up his window. Joseph is going to talk to the policewoman who has pulled us over because she spotted me taking photos along a road in Lagos, Nigeria. With a tinny thud of the Corolla's door, he's gone, and I'm left in loud silence.

The unfolding drama has drawn a crowd, eager for a diversion from the monotony of waiting for an odd job or selling items as small as a single cigarette. The onlookers seem more curious than hostile, but I'm not about to get out and test my theory. Embarrassed by their stares, I gaze at the road throttled with semi-trailers waiting to enter the Lagos Port Complex.

I was taking random pictures of the roadside, a boil of trucks, motorcycles, three-wheeled taxis, peddlers of everything from corn-cobs to car parts, and women walking with beanpole backs to balance massive baskets of goods on their heads, but the cop seems to think I have a sinister motive, I suppose because I'm a foreigner. "I want to know who you are, who is behind you," she told Joseph.

Nerves grip my stomach, but I remain calm. As a foreign correspondent, I ran into similar situations in Latin America. So far, I've never had to call the U.S. Embassy for help.

I arrived in Nigeria the previous night. Lagos is the second stop on a pilgrimage to retrace the earliest years of my childhood, the ones that predate my memory, but I've heard about from my parents my whole life. It's a zigzag of a journey. I lived in seven countries by age thirteen. My mother was an English nurse and my father a mining engineer from New Zealand who met in a Zambian copper mining town. When Mum was eight months pregnant with me, they left Africa for New Zealand where I was born. Three weeks later, we moved to Fiji. We then lived in Sweden, England, Nigeria, New Zealand, Australia and the United States.

My parents thought it would be grand and glamorous to raise their children as citizens of the world. But for me, it has meant a lifetime living in limbo. I am from everywhere and thus nowhere. I have three nationalities yet belong to no country. I can relate to almost anybody, but few can relate to me. I experienced an extraordinarily rich, stimulating childhood, yet it has brought me deep loneliness in its singularity. I have felt conflicted about my childhood my entire life. Perhaps this trip will bring me a resolution.

We arrived in Lagos in 1964 when I was not even two years old for Dad's job with a Swedish multinational and left in 1966. We lived in a block of flats on Rycroft Road, which I know thanks to Mum's notation on the back of a small black and white photo showing Dad holding my sister outside the apartment. I hired Joseph through a friend of a friend to take me there.

I'd taken four photos en route when a traffic warden forced Joseph to stop. Then two policewomen appeared on either side of the Corolla demanding to know why I was "snapping."

"I will handle this," Joseph said and turned to the officer in his window. "What is the offense?"

The other policewoman was rapping on my window and pointing at the phone in my lap. I ignored her since Joseph was in charge. She tried the door handle. I was suddenly glad it was broken.

"Let me see the camera." The policewoman on Joseph's side poked a forefinger through the window.

"It is not a crime to take photos," he said. "She wasn't taking photos of you."

"The camera."

I handed him the phone.

"Scroll to the pictures," she ordered. Joseph swiped the screen to the slightly fuzzy photos. The other policewoman joined her, and they huddled at the window scrutinizing the pictures like blood splatters at a murder scene.

"I can delete them," I said. "They're really nothing."

They ignored me. The second officer flashed a finger at a photo. "I know that man!" She disappeared.

Joseph has been gone for a while now, and it's stifling inside the Corolla. I twist in my seat to see what's going on. Joseph is pleading his case to the lead cop, who's not buying it. Then I hear buzzing. Outside my window, a man crouches at the front wheel with a dusty machine. He's inflating the tire. He duckwalks to the rear tire and does the same.

Joseph returns, grim-faced. The rear door opens. To my surprise, the policewoman slides into the back seat, followed by the man from my photo, the one the other policewoman said she knew. She must have fetched him.

No one says anything so I don't ask where we're going but I assume it's the police station. After pushing through the traffic choke, we turn onto a lumpy dirt road and stop outside a low-slung, concrete building where several Jeeps with police insignia are parked.

Inside, the policewoman ushers us into an office where a tall man cuts a smart figure in an immaculate white "senator suit," Nigeria's traditional cotton tunic-style top with matching fitted-leg pants. I presume he's the local police chief.

"What is going on here?" he says.

"She was videoing." The policewoman points at me.

He looks puzzled, then Joseph explains our mission to find Rycroft Road.

The chief turns to me. "I want to hear from you, Madame."

"I wasn't videoing. I took four photos of the street to have a memory of the area because I lived on Rycroft Road when I was a baby." I find the old picture, which I had uploaded onto my phone, and hand it to him.

He smiles. "Is that your father?" he says.

"Yes."

"Is that you?"

There's no point in complicating matters by saying it's actually my sister. "Yes." He swipes through the photos I took of the street. "I wasn't taking pictures of anything specific. It's just to remember the area I once lived in."

He looks at the policewoman. "She was just snapping to have a memory of where she lived. They are always snapping. Look, selfies. They love selfies." He swishes through the photos with mild amusement. "You are free to snap. You can snap me if you like." He hands me back the phone. I have been exonerated.

He turns to Joseph. "If you had told the officer this to begin with, we wouldn't be here. You must respect the police."

Joseph mumbles an apology. The chief gives a dismissive wave. We're free to go.

We drive the policewoman and the other man back to the intersection, then head to Rycroft Road. We laugh about the incident. "It wasn't so funny a little while ago," Joseph says.

I ask him what the tire inflation was for. "They deflated the tires so I couldn't drive away. Then I have to pay to have them inflated again. That's what I was arguing about."

We turn into Rycroft Road. We drive slowly, then near the end of the street, I spot a three-story building, white with grey trim. It's surrounded by a high wall and metal gate, but through the gap between the wall and gate, I make out distinctive concrete ledges that jut over the windows, as in the photo.

"I think that's it!"

Joseph reverses, and we get out. Joseph explains my story to a security guard and asks if I can take a photo. The guard opens the gate, and we enter. The place is tidy, the paint fresh.

I place my palm against the wall of the ground-floor flat that we may have lived in. At that moment, I claim the childhood that has often seemed the stuff of story more than reality. For those of us who grew up among far-flung cultures, our childhoods lack physicality. They become Brigadoon-like, existing solely in the mist of memory. It's inevitable.

When we move, we must focus on adapting to a new setting that demands we molt our past self and mold ourselves to fit the present. As a child, I had to change shape so many times I never really knew who I was, nor did it matter. I had to belong, so I had to discard the things that made me different and be the same as everyone else.

Finding this building is a touchpoint to how my upbringing shaped my true self, the one who became a foreign correspondent and lived in three more countries as an adult, who finds change, travel and adventure exhilarating, who is endlessly fascinated by difference.

Joseph snaps a picture of me, triumphant at locating this tiny scrap of my history that I've come halfway around the globe to find. It was absolutely worth the hassle to come here.

A TALE OF TWO REUNIONS
MICHAEL P. KUSEN

Over seventy years ago, during World War II, two American soldiers had a chance meeting in a little town in eastern France. They were in different military units, one coming from the north and one coming from the south, that happened to converge at the same time at the same place. When they met, they smiled and embraced greeting each other. It was a little respite from the harshness and daily drudgery of the war. But more than that, it was a minor miracle because they were brothers, William and Steve Kusen, from New York City.

William and Steve grew up in uptown Manhattan on Madison Avenue along with another brother, Joseph, who served in the Pacific. William was the oldest and was drafted into the Army in 1941. Shortly thereafter, Steve was also drafted into the Army and later Joseph was drafted into the Army Air Force, which was the fledgling unit that became the US Airforce in 1947.

William was assigned to the 152 Signal Company of the 12th Armored Division (a tank corps nicknamed the "Hellcats"). He reached the rank of Technical Sergeant as a radio repair specialist. His unit crossed the English Channel in early November of 1944, and established an assembly area in Auffay, France by mid-November. Allied military forces were moving swiftly across France and in early December the Hellcats had reached a staging area for an offensive into Germany. Steve Kusen was assigned to the Fifth Army's 45th Signal Corps nicknamed the "Thunderbirds." His unit had come up through Italy into France. It was there in the town of Luneville in the province of Lorraine, about 100 miles from the Rhine River and the city of Strasbourg, Germany where the two brothers met.

William and Steve hadn't seen each other for more than two years since they both had furloughs in New York City. Now it seemed like a gift from fate that these two brothers should have this chance meeting just before the allied forces final assault into Germany. And the two brothers made the most of their time together in Luneville. Their reminiscing was enhanced by their singing as William played the mandolin and they even managed to share a meal with some of the local residents of Luneville. Yet unknown to them, Hitler was about to put up his last ferocious attempt to defend Germany. The German High Command was planning the "Ardennes Offensive" or as we Americans came to call it, "The Battle of the Bulge." Fortunately, both brothers survived the final days of those European battles. And remarkably all three brothers came home uninjured and were noted for meritorious service.

After the war each brother resumed his civilian life eventually marrying and having a family: William had a son and two daughters, Steve had two sons, and Joseph had three sons and two daughters. They were living the "American Dream" of the post war prosperity – each bought a home and moved out of the congested city apartment life that they grew up in. But as they uprooted themselves they also drifted apart so that over the years their children (ten cousins) grew up barely knowing each other. And with the passing of time, one by one each brother died: William in 1967 in New York City, Joseph in 1981 on Long Island, New York and Steve died in 1993 in Fayetteville, Tennessee. With Steve Kusen's death, the last parental link for the ten cousins was gone.

But perhaps another minor miracle could happen for the Kusen family, like that chance meeting in Luneville, France, all those years ago. And that is what happened when Elisha Kusen (son of Steve) picked up the phone to try to find his cousin Michael (son of William).

Elisha grew up in Tennessee where he still currently lives with his wife and son. In mid-March 1997 Elisha was in New York City on business when he decided to try to find out if Michael was still living in New York. After a few calls and messages Elisha's hopes were answered when Michael returned his call.

"Hello," Elisha said in a slight southern accent.

"Is this Elisha Kusen?" Michael asked.

"Yes, it is."

"My God," replied Michael, "I haven't seen you since you were about eight years old. I have a vague memory of you running around on the grass in our backyard. How old are you now?"

"Forty-two," Elisha answered.

"You're forty-two – I'm fifty. I can't believe how much time has gone by."

The reminiscing went on and the next day the two estranged cousins had lunch in a Brooklyn restaurant. That's when Michael learned that Elisha had also contacted their cousin Peter, the eldest son of their Uncle Joseph.

Peter was living in Newark, New Jersey with his wife and three children. Peter had invited Elisha to his home that coming Saturday. And from Peter's invitation, an impromptu cousin's reunion began to form in the next few days as Peter contacted his brothers and sisters.

So on a sunny Saturday afternoon in March, Peter Kusen and his wife Patty hosted a cousin's reunion filled with stories and questions and the full dynamics of a family rediscovering itself after many lost years. There was laughter and the exchanging of photos and addresses and a new generation of children running about. There was talk of recording a family history and invitations and plans for other gatherings. It is a very heart-warming experience to rekindle the feeling of belonging to an extended family. To look into the faces of cousins, after such a long absence, and see the resemblances of long-gone uncles and aunts creates a tender bond. I know because my name is Michael Kusen and the next reunion was at my house.

CONTACT INITIATION
JANET MAIKA'I RUDOLPH

For this is my message, the message of a dancer.
Within your being, within your mind and your living body,
lies a world of joy and power.
Ruth St. Denis (*Wisdom Comes Dancing*)

PART 1

I have always considered myself a dancer. This, despite the fact that I
have no particular talent. My body tends toward short and stocky.
My *grande jetes* barely get off the ground. I've never been able to do a
split. And yet in my head, I use my body with a dancer's awareness to
move through the world. No one else can see it, but I can feel it deep
inside my muscles and bones.

I had forgotten the roots of this part of my life. But after my
mother died in 2018, I happened upon the Dances of Universal
Peace (DUP). Although founded in a Sufi tradition by Murshid
Samuel Lewis, they are multicultural, and multi-spiritual. The
Dances involve a song or chant, often in a sacred language such as
Hebrew, Arabic, Hindi, and Hawaiian. The languages are sacred
because their words contain vibrational essences we can feel
throughout our bodies. Along with the songs, there are choreo-
graphed dances to enhance those vibrations with body movement. I
knew this feeling; I couldn't place why at the time, but I just knew I
loved working with them.

The beauty of using our whole bodies along with breath and voice spoke to me like nothing else and awakened my heart. The dances are done in circles, sometimes with partners, so the rhythmic essence grows stronger as we move together in community.

One day, my friend and dance leader, Mariam, referenced Ruth St. Denis's book *Wisdom Comes Dancing*. Samuel Lewis credited Ruth St. Denis with inspiring him to create the dances. St. Denis was an early modern dancer, one of the mavericks along with Isadora Duncan, Martha Graham, and Helen Tamiris. I was hit with a lightning bolt of recognition. I had taken modern dance classes when I was in my teens. When Mariam spoke the words of St. Denis out loud, I heard them as if my dance teacher were whispering into my ear in the present day. Yet, it had been 50 years since I took those classes.

My childhood dance teacher was Dvo Margenau. She taught modern dance as it was conceived at its inception, and which harmonized well in the hippie period of the 1960s. Dvo herself had been one of those early modern dancers, performing along with Martha Graham and Helen Tamiris in the 1930s.

Dvo was a soloist with Helen Tamiris' company for 12 years. At only five feet tall, she stood out as a powerhouse. As my dance teacher some 30 years later, she remained a force to be reckoned with. Ballerinas soar as they launch themselves into the air, taking flight and making gravity disappear. Dvo and other modern dancers were creatures of the earth, stomping on the land, with an intimate connection. This isn't to mean that they couldn't do amazing leaps and jumps, but when they did, they would land in a gravity-laden world. In fact, while graceful ballerinas embody a world without gravity, modern dancers embrace it.

Ballerinas toes are forever pointed, the line of the leg so important to the idealized beauty of its form. In our modern dance class, our toes were flexed, a rebellion against such an ideal, a revolt against grace, even while being graceful (but only at times and by choice). We never sought after an ideal, it was honesty of expression that was valued above all else. And along the way, we honored our connection to the earth, our movement through space, the rhythm of our lives reflected in our bodies. The tools we used were the intake of breath, the extension of a crooked leg, the sweep of an arm with a sharp elbow, clawing our way along the earth on bended knee, reaching for the sky with fingers askew.

When our parents came in to watch, improvisation was the prominent showcase of our work. The point was to express ourselves warts, bruises and all. If we were feeling ugly, sad, traumatized or fearful we were encouraged to express it as much as when we were feeling joyful and loving. All emotions and feelings were encouraged, respected and expressed.

This was quite the revelation for me. I had grown up in an alcoholic, violent family. Abuse makes you invisible. It takes away your voice. It is downright dangerous to express your own thoughts and opinions. A cloak of invisibility comes to feel like a shield of protection. It may not have always worked but any illusion of safety is welcomed, even craved.

Yet here was Dvo creating an actual haven, a place to be honest and to express myself. A place to channel my rage, my loathing, my shame. It felt safe because it was camouflaged. It could only be seen and understood by those with eyes to see. Hidden in plain sight, I could let go, give free reign to the fullness of me.

I had forgotten all of it until reading *Wisdom Comes Dancing*. Here's another piece about abuse. We become so practiced in forgetting the painful hard parts of our lives that we also lose the good parts. Dvo was a good part, and I realized I had forgotten too much. How could I find her memory? How could I reclaim that part of my life?

To do that, I had to become a detective. There were a few scant mentions of Dvo Margenau on the internet. She was born in 1910 and died in 1981. There were brief mentions of her as a dance teacher and with nothing about her earlier career.

I remembered that she had a home in Stockbridge, MA, home of Jacob's Pillow, founded by Ted Shawn, husband of Ruth St. Denis. My first thought was to see if they had a library of archives. But, then I realized I had a resource much closer to home, the Lincoln Center Library of the Performing Arts in New York City. I wrote to them and their librarian answered me almost immediately. He told me there was no mention of a Dvo Margenau but there were many folders of newspaper clippings surrounding the career of Helen Tamiris. I told him my story of Dvo and we settled on a strategy of looking for her through the Tamiris folders from the 1930s. That was when Dvo would have been in the prime of her dancing career. I made an appointment to visit the following week.

The library staff was very thorough. They had a stack of folders already prepared based on my requests. Each folder, sitting on the shelving behind the librarian's desk, was labeled by a span of years. They allowed me to look through them one at a time. It took 3 or 4 folders, but I finally hit the nugget I was searching for. It was a program for a dance recital of Helen Tamiris' company in 1937 that listed the names of the dancers. One of those dancers was Dvo Seron. My heart began to race. Since Dvo is not a common name. I knew it had to be her. Here was my first tangible evidence of Dvo in her early years.

But there was more. There was also a photo of the Tamiris dancers in 1936 with the caption, *"Vigor and freedom mark this dance by Tamiris and her group."*

The dancers were not named but I knew from the chills running up and down my spine that I was looking at Dvo. Her energy was unmistakable, her face was lit up with light and exuberance (2nd from left). But there were two problems in being sure. It had been over 50 years since I'd last seen Dvo and I couldn't trust my memory as to what she looked like. And second, when I knew her, she was in her late 50s and in this picture, she was in her 20s. I didn't trust those goosebumps still dotting my spine. With permission from the library, I took the photo above with my phone.

CONTACT INITIATION – PART 2

I was exhausted when I got home from the Performing Arts Library but my craving for more information had only been whetted. I couldn't wait to see if more could be found. Heading straight to my keyboard, I typed in a search for "Dvo Seron." And, there she was! I found a photo of Tamiris' dance company with dancers named, including Dvo. As in the library, I could feel my excitement rise; here was my first confirmed photo of her. But again, I had a problem, I couldn't be sure which of the dancers was Dvo. To add to the confusion, the caption listed 7 dancers yet there are only 6 in the photo.

(Helen Tamiris, center, with fellow dancers Augusta Gassner, Dvo Seron, Ailes Gilmour, Marion Appell, and Lulu Morris, 1937. Photo courtesy of the Library of Congress.)

At this point I felt like an addict and information was the drug that I craved. There were so many tantalizing clues, but the substance still remained out of reach. I was tired, frustrated and began going down internet rabbit holes. When I began a search at a questionable website, my screen froze with a message that my computer had been infected with a virus that needed "Microsoft" to fix. Or maybe it was "Mucrusoft." I was instructed to send bitcoin to their service department. Perfect for my mood. A hacking company of uncertain name thwarting my efforts. I realized I needed a new tactic, so I shut my computer and went to bed.

The next morning when I turned on my computer, the frozen screen and bitcoin request were gone. Huzzah, a new day to find new clues. I wracked my brain trying to glean any shred of information that would lead me back to Dvo. Dvo's husband Ernest was a prominent sculptor so I figured there had to be more I could find, perhaps in their local Stockbridge town newspaper. I wrote to the Stockbridge library to see what they might have. Once again, the librarians came through. What they had was thin but key. Ernest's obituary listed their son Eric whom I had vaguely remembered from the 1960s. He was about 15 years older than I. From the information the librarian gave me, I was able to find him from an internet search. He is a sports psychologist who is still working. I called the number. When he picked up the phone, I held my breath.

"Hello," I said tentatively. "Is this Eric Margenau?"

"It is," he answered.

I introduced myself and told him, "I took dance lessons with your mother back in the 1960s and 70s."

There was a pause on the phone. Was he sorting through his own emotions? Wondering if I was a crazy person contacting him?

I continued with a thought that I had forgotten but just popped into my head, "Your mom and mine were friends. My mom's name was Betty Levin."

He broke his silence. "I remember your mom," he said. Did I detect warmth in his voice?

We began to reminisce. It was like finding a long-lost family member. He told me that Seron was Dvo's stage name. I emailed him the two photos I had. He confirmed that the woman I identified in the 1st photo is indeed his mom. He also identified his mother in the 2nd photo (lower left). After learning about this, I contacted the Performing Arts Library to see if they were interested in this information. They were and I sent it to them for their own files.

With this, my journey into my past took another unexpected turn. Dvo had not only opened my eyes to personal expression through our bodies, but she was now a conduit to my mother, the good parts of my mother. My mother never abused me, but she also never protected me, and she looked away when things grew too painful. To her dying day, she could never acknowledge nor discuss the violence of my childhood.

But here, this was a completely different mother than the one I had been remembering. She had created the circumstances where I was able to take these lessons with Dvo. She set up a whole after-school enrichment program with different instructors teaching the arts. My mother had an eye for culture and talent. Two local world-famous artists, Jacob Landau and Ted Shapiro, gave classes in art. Robert Wilson, who wrote, produced and directed avant-garde plays, taught theatre and Dvo Margenau taught dance. In the often turbulent relationship I had with my mother, this was a noted exception and one that I have come to treasure.

On some level, my mother must have known that we could never talk honestly to each other. Keeping secrets breaks the bonds of communication and abuse is one of the darkest ones possible. I was closed off and holding in deep pain. My mother was clearly feeling guilt and shame and dealing with the family's abuse would have destroyed her marriage. Her marriage was destroyed anyway, but she didn't become aware of that for a very long time. Yet in this chaos and dysfunction, my mother did something spectacular and in doing so she was weaving an invisible lifeline for me to find when I was ready.

It took me 50 years, but that lifeline she wove so long ago has grown to become a bright shining bridge.

It is a titanic shift of perspective for me to have found evidence 3 years after my mother had died, that there had been a love of sorts between us two.

With that, it has been easier for me to feel compassion about her own life woundings. She had her own demons surrounding mother issues. Her own mother had died when she was 2. Her stepmother, my grandma, was a loving woman but by the time she stepped into the family, my mother had been living with other relatives for many years. By all accounts, my mother was loved very much by all her relatives, but it had to have been challenging for them to care for a motherless toddler and confusing for her that she found herself living in so many different homes.

My own mother could not stop the abuse nor openly express her love for me. On some level, she knew her limitations and yet she did what she could. As I said, spectacular. She gave me art. She gave me dance. She left behind a trail so I could follow it back to the better angels of her heart. And that has also opened the pathways of healing for me.

I still love dance and go to performances whenever I can. I still do the Dances of Universal Peace. My own body is older and stiffer now, so I have to adjust myself to my abilities when I express myself through movement. Our bodies are the foundation of how we experience life on this earth, and I treasure that I learned this lesson early, even though I did forget it for many years. It's come back as a tidal wave to change my life for the better in uncountable ways.

Contact Initiation is the point in the body which begins a dance movement. It can be the contraction of stomach muscles, the tapping of toes, the flick of chin. All subsequent movement flows out of that initial movement. I find myself wondering about that dynamic spark that began this story. Is it in the present day when I first found the words of St. Denis and went looking for Dvo? Is it when I found Eric as a link to my past? Was it back in my teen-age years when Dvo first taught me to express myself so profoundly? Or was it when my mother looked so desperately for alternative ways to express her love for me?

Each step of this journey could not have existed without the others. It feels to me as if time collapsed to create a holistic narrative even though the fragments appear, on the outside, to be 50 years apart. And for the first time in my life, I can say that I feel whole.

AUNT JANE
HEIDI NEWNAM

"This is a piece of your past", she said as she handed my mom an object wrapped in tissue paper. Mom sat on the couch looking at the tissue paper and smiling. Her newly discovered half- sister Jane, was sitting next to her. Jane inched closer and unwrapped the paper from the object mom was holding while guarding it from falling to the floor.

"We were never allowed to touch these growing up. Each one of us kids got one when we became adults. When my sister died, I got hers and now I am giving it to you", Jane said.

Mom studied the beautiful crystal glass with the initial of her maiden name etched into it.

It took almost two years from the time my sister submitted her DNA test until she connected with our aunt. Things moved quickly once the contact was made. We always knew our grandfather's name and that he lived in a neighboring state. That was really all our mom ever knew about him. Jane didn't know a thing about her dad having any other children until she was in her 40's and he was dying. She wasn't given much information beyond having a sister she never knew.

I sat across from my mom and new found aunt, blinking back tears. Mom's dementia was pretty advanced and it was hard to tell how much she was comprehending. The feelings from loss and gain mixed within me.

"Do you have any pictures from your childhood?" Jane asked my mom.

Boxes of old photos were placed on the card table in front of the couch where the two of them sat. I watched Jane thoughtfully interact with mom, giving her undivided attention. I studied Jane's features for any resemblance to us. Jane asked questions about the pictures and patiently waded through the convoluted answers that my mom gave. The initial answers were always better than the answers to the follow up questions.

The last time I went through those photos with my mom, she showed me a picture of her mother and said "she looks like a monkey". I waited for her to do it again with her sister, but she didn't.

I think Jane is very brave for being vulnerable and traveling two hours for this meeting. Can a person have a kind of survivor's guilt in a situation like this? She made the cut and my mom didn't where their father was concerned.

Jane shared pictures of her family, and told us things about her father. When he was dying, his wife blurted out that he wasn't perfect, and he had another child. That's how Jane found out about my mom. My grandfather had a cat that he loved, which his jealous wife renamed with something to express her disdain for the cat. If this is any indication of how my mom would have been treated, I think it was better that she was kept away. I am thankful that my mom can't think to ask questions.

"I'm glad you had a good childhood and people that loved you" Jane said to my mom.

The pictures of my mom's childhood do not capture what growing up without her father actually meant to her; a lifelong struggle with shame, sadness, and anger. Decades later she is still brought to tears when someone unknowingly asks her about her family history and she tells them she never knew her father.

Those pictures are of people smiling and dressed nicely. Prom gowns, fur coats, and no hairs out of place. What the pictures don't show is a mother sitting at a kitchen table, crying as she explains to her young daughter that she never knew her father. What the pictures don't show is a wounded woman lashing out at her kids, gaslighting and guilting them - tearing them down with her words. It was universally accepted in our house that my mom had a rough childhood and therefore should be excused for hurting us. It was our responsibility to tend to the feelings that she could not.

The same story repeated for years from a mother with tears in her eyes to a daughter helpless to fix the situation. My memory recalls my mom's stories in short choppy clips like a spliced home movie - "I never knew my father". "My mother wouldn't tell me anything". "My aunt was the one that told me his name". "He lived in the next state". Stories bound together with shame, embarrassment, and anger; Catholic school nuns, her mother and step father drunk walking up the sidewalk, going to live with her grandmother.

I'm no psychologist, but I suspect even psychologists aren't very good at helping people they have intense emotional connections with. My mother was a child at a time when not as much was known about childhood psychology and having a father that left your mother carried a lot of shame. It is understood today that adverse childhood experiences have a significant, negative impact on the life of the child. Maybe my mom just had a mental health disorder and we made excuses because she never knew her father. Maybe she had a mental health disorder because of her adverse childhood experiences from not knowing her father. I will never know.

Before consumer DNA testing was a thing, I searched the internet for information on my grandfather. I called the number of someone I found that I thought might be his wife, that I now know was one of his daughters. My heart was pounding so hard that I could feel it in my throat when I placed the call. I was relieved when I reached a recording stating the phone had been disconnected. Maybe a man that left his tiny baby wasn't the kind of person worth knowing. I thought we would find out he was a jerk, and gave up my search. Now that I know some things about him, I don't think he was.

Growing up, I had things that many other children did not; new clothes, toys, a swimming pool, a pony, an intact nuclear family that ate meals together and went visiting grandparents on weekends, "the belt", and more eggshells to walk on than a commercial egg farm.

One winter when I was about twelve years old, mom called for me to come in from out in the snow. I remembered that I had to finish something so I told her I would be there in a minute. I was met at the door when I came in, blindsided by a woman with clenched teeth. I was beaten with my dad's leather belt until large red welts appeared on my skin. I should have come when she called. Even the dog knew that much. I had beatings before this, and often felt that I deserved them. This time I was certain that I didn't. Living in an environment like this is what I imagine walking through a landmine must feel like. My mere existence seemed to enrage her, and she didn't attempt to hide it.

Nothing was off limits when it came to her anger, not even my slumber birthday party. Who could possibly expect a room full of giggling girls stuffed with pizza and ice cream to be quiet? When we were supposed to be settling down for the night, my sister came into the room and started telling us scary stories. Her boyfriend hid outside and rattled the window, causing us to scream, making any kind of winding down difficult. The giggling and chatter carried on after lights out. My mom expected us to fall asleep and be quiet once the lights were out, and when we didn't, she reacted. Her very distinct tread as she slammed her feet down with force told me I was about to be sorry. She erupted into the room where me and my friends were, swiftly grabbed me by the hair in front of all of them and dragged me up the stairs. I cried myself to sleep in my own bed while all of my friends slept downstairs.

Decades later, my mom was commenting in an oddly prideful way that her daughters only ever wanted one slumber party. She was implying that we didn't need those sorts of things. Sarcastically, I said "yeah, well I got drug up the steps by my hair that's why I never wanted another one". She stopped talking to me for days after that. By this time, I was a grown woman with a child of my own and much less injured by her tantrums. I realized that she would never be the kind of person I want her to be so I adapted to fit the relationship, to keep the peace - what I had been taught to do all of my life but never could until then. I found other adult women to grow with such as my mother in law. My mom was jealous of her. Once she saw a picture of my mother in law in my daughter's bedroom and cried.

Like it is for a lot of people, my teen years were rough. Already having years of fearing my mom under my belt, I turned angry. I wished she was dead. Realizing nothing I did or didn't do protected me from my mom's anger, I stopped trying to follow the rules. When this happened, I was sent to someone to help me be controllable again. The psychiatrist that tried to help me looked like Alfred Hitchcock. He had the most amusing way of saying cottage cheese and I would often ask him to say it. I think the subject must have come up during a discussion of nutrition or something. Our relationship ended the day he suggested to my mom that she had something to do with my issues.

Shortly afterward, I began seeing a younger psychologist. He offered a safe place where I could say anything without fear of retaliation. He recorded meditations on a cassette tape for me. I liked him and felt uplifted and validated by the support he gave. Misunderstanding the positive changes in me, my mother accused us of having an inappropriate relationship, and I never saw him again.

Despite our past, me and my mom were able to have a pretty good adult relationship and grew closer. I had worked through the hurt and didn't make it a theme of our future, which is probably why I cried for days after her Alzheimer's diagnosis. I didn't want this for her. It's not uncommon for people with Alzheimer's to become paranoid. As the disease progressed, that's exactly what happened to my mom. She became abusive with anyone who contradicted her. This side to her was the same abusive side that came out when she felt disrespected before she had Alzheimer's, reopening every emotional wound that I thought had healed. Fortunately, she is now on medications and the paranoia and aggressiveness have gone away. I suspect the medications would have helped her long before the Alzheimer's diagnosis. The positive thing about her current mental state is that she is happy and much harder to offend. I guess the part of her brain that told her she needed to hurt others has died. My poor tortured mom seems to finally be at peace.

Parentification is the term used to describe when the child takes on the role of the parent. Looking back, I think that is what happened to me where my mom's emotions were concerned. The combination of hurting for her and fearing her made my mom's happiness a big concern of mine. I tried to help her by being a good listener and censoring what I said, but I didn't do a very good job because she always seemed to get angry. Avoidance didn't work either because she was bothered by me spending too much time in my room, or became accusatory if I was out with my friends. I was constantly worried about how my mom was feeling, and trying my best to keep her from being set off. Dealing with her now is similar to how it was back when I was a child, and I find that I instinctively know what to do.

Finding my grandfather represents fixing my mom. All of my life I hoped she would find him, and that finding him would heal her brokenness. Finding out about him will have to be sufficient. It's the next best thing to finding him, and it gives closure to my mom's life-long torment.

It's bittersweet, my mom finding her sister when she's lost the ability to fully comprehend it. I will comprehend for her. I am a steward of my mom's past. I will take in the gravity and meaning of gaining this new family member for my mom. I will weave my grand-father's family tree into our own, something my mom cannot do for herself. I will have a relationship with my aunt, in my mom's place, and I will heal—for both of us.

LOST AND FOUND
JOAN FOOR

My brother Les and I were anxious with anticipation for supper as Dad carved the twenty pound turkey. Mother slowly stirred in small amounts of flour to the turkey drippings, hoping for a non-lumpy gravy. Grand-pap and Grandma sat in the parlor, glancing occasionally at the small black and white table television waiting for Dad to say, "Come and Get it!" This was Dad's big day. He's so proud to provide a Thanksgiving meal to his parents. For many years, it was over the hill to Grand-pap's house we went. Mother and Dad wanted everything to be perfect. It was!

"The turkey is moist," Dad remarked with a happy grin from ear to ear. The happiest I've seen him look in months. Of course, when the turkey is juicy that's a big deal, a major concern when Mother and Dad bake a turkey. My brother and I stuffed ourselves. As usual, it was like we never got enough to eat, which was never the case. With our mouths full, we listened to Grand-pap and Grandma express how everything tasted from the cranberry jewel salad to the baked corn taken hot from the oven. After second helpings, everyone agreed we would save the pumpkin pie with whipped cream for later. Grand-pap was a great storyteller. He started to repeat the story about being an orphan until two tall spinster sisters adopted him at twelve. They needed help to manage their old run-down farm in Groundhog Valley. Grand-pap happened to be tall and appeared strong so they adopted him. He was happy to have a home and he learned quickly how to milk the two jersey cows, plow and plant the fields with Nell, a worn-out older horse, and wooden plow. In addition, he tended to the livestock, the chickens and learned to slop the hogs after meals.

His eyes sparkled as he spoke. He would look over at Les and I when speaking. I believe it was to ensure he had our attention. Always pointing a reference to how easy our lives were compared to the olden days during his childhood. "When Myrtle and Pearl, the two sisters, let me go fishing, I hooked up Nell to the buggy and traveled over the mountain ridge to the Juniata River. It took the better half of a day to get there but it was worth it. Hauling in a sucker fish weighing over a pound was fun. It had begun to be a skill to land one without breaking my line. I continued to please the sisters with my catch, especially in the spring when the river was high and muddy. In those days, we caught eel, salmon, catfish, and fall fish along with large suckers. Both you kids are aware I fished along the same river you do today that flows in front of your cottage, right?"

"Yes, Grand-pap. I caught a big sucker fish last March, remember?" I blurted out.

"By George you're right, 'Windjammer'." Grand-pap nicknamed me 'Windjammer' because he said I talk too much. "You were so excited you let your line go slack and almost lost it," he added. "You kids have no idea how hard it was to get around when your Grand-pap was your age. Your Grand-pap had to ride horseback or hook up old Nell to the buggy, like he said. He lived over the mountain range not far from our cottage. Last summer, I showed both of you a narrow steep overgrown dirt road leading off to the left that heads over the ridge into Groundhog Valley. Your Grand-pap traveled that road from when he was adopted until well into his twenties He had to work hard on a small farm on the other side of the ridge."

"Yes, Dad. I remember. I asked if you could drive us up there to see where Grand-pap lived. You said the road was too rough and probably our car wouldn't make it," Les went on.

"That's correct, son. Perhaps, I can rent a Willys Jeep in the near future and take you kids up that road to see the valley. It's covered with large farms now." Dad said.

"Russ, you did know the narrow one lane dirt road you travel to your cottage is the same one I traveled by horse and buggy? It is some wider now to allow milk trucks from nearby dairy farms to be able to pass other vehicles in certain spots. Cars have slipped off the edge of that dirt road over the years. The lucky ones were stopped by trees half way down the embankment, others plunged forty feet below into the river," Grand-pap remarked.

"I know how dangerous it is, Pop. I had forgotten you traveled over the same road by horse and buggy years before. Tell your grandchildren how when in your twenties you went about finding out you had a sister.

"Grand-pap, I'm always scared when Dad drives around those curves. I close my eyes when we are on the outside edge of the road and I can see the river below," I said.

"I'm not surprised, honey, there were times I was scared myself. I may have told you kids some of this story before. Well, Myrtle and Pearl, the sisters who raised me, knew nothing about my background. They adopted me from an agency in Hagerstown, Maryland. I sent a letter of inquiry and heard back I could request a copy of my birth certificate there. I kept after the sisters to let me travel to Hagerstown to the Hall of Records. Reluctantly, in my early twenties they loaned me the horse and buggy. After several days, I reached the city hall. The county clerk was very helpful. Thank heavens I knew my birth date, at least I thought I did. I was shocked when the clerk said, "You were born with a twin sister. She came a few minutes after you. According to our records her name was Anna. Tears came to my eyes. To think I had a sister! She could tell me about who my mother and father were. There were so many questions I had about my family. Where were they and how could I find them? I asked for an address or how I could find this Anna. They gave me the address they had on record. I fed and watered Nell then rode out to the outskirts of Hagerstown to find my sister. When I arrived at that address I was told she had married a man by the name of Dick Dermer and moved to a small tenant farm on the opposite side of town. I sought a bed and breakfast for the night and boarded old Nell."

"Grandpap, your sister was the aunt who showed up at the cottage with her husband and two grandkids last summer, right? The one who had a big swollen neck and wore a little white hat," Les offered.

"Yes, that was your Great Aunt Anna, my twin sister. Her huge neck was due to an enlarged thyroid gland, a goiter. When we were young, not everyone got enough iodized salt in their diets. To continue, I didn't sleep all night worrying. Maybe my parents would turn out to be bad people or in jail."

"Why, would you think your parents would be criminals, Grandpap? I asked.

"I was scared. I didn't know what to expect. After all, they gave us both up for adoption. Why would they do that? I went to bed and could not sleep worrying about what to expect the next day."

"I don't remember what you told us about them. Were they really bad like you thought?" I asked.

"No, not really. But I found out very little about them. I got up early, watered and fed Nell and headed with the buggy to the new address. I traveled a road leading through groomed farmland and stopped at one farm for directions. The plowed fields were lined up so straight I was amazed, not like the crooked plowing I was capable of with Nell. It was mostly flat land with gradual slopes. The farm houses sat farther back from the fields surrounded by fir and maple trees for shade. There were shock piles here and there where the wheat was stacked butt end down in neat rows ready for winter. I finally arrived at a small farm house painted white with a red barn out back. I was a nervous wreck not knowing what my sister would be like. I rapped on the screen door. A short plump woman wearing a long black faded out dress covered by a white linen apron and small white cap pushed open the screen door."

"What can I do to help you sir?" She said in a hoarse, and raspy voice.

"Are you Dick Dermer's wife, Anna?" I asked sheepishly.

"Yes, who do I have the pleasure of talking with?" She asked with a kind smile.

"Our eyes met straight on. It was as though she sensed who I was before I could speak. 'I'm Leslie Border,' I stretched out my hand, my voice quivered. 'Your brother.' I could barely get the words out. There I stood, her long lost twin brother. Without hesitation, she kicked the door open and reached out with open arms. I leaned down wrapped my arms around her, crying out loud. We hugged for a long while. She grabbed hold of my arm, her hand was rough like sandpaper, undoubtedly from hard work. She led me into the parlor."

"When inside, she used the corner of her apron to wipe away the tears running down her face. We sat in front of a natural stone fireplace that covered the entire wall. Neither one of us knew anything about our mother, father or each other. She explained it hadn't been that long ago when she found out our mother was unwed and died a few days after our birth with pneumonia. Since all she knew was her adopted parents, she was happy and saw no reason to search for her real parents. However, when she applied for a marriage license, she felt the need to inquire about her real background. Her adopted mother was able to tell her what little she knew about her birth mother. But, she knew nothing about our father. It was strange her adopted parents never knew about me, a twin brother. Your Great Aunt Anna was lucky to be adopted as a newborn into a wonderful Mennonite family. I expressed my concern about her swollen neck as I was about to depart. She assured me it had been evaluated and was too dangerous to be operated on."

"That must have been quite a day, Pop. I was glad your sister found the cottage. You gave them great directions. I was so glad to meet her, the husband and grandkids. She shared her upbringing and the excitement about the day you showed up unexpectedly. I saw how much you resemble each other Pop. It's a small wonder I guess, after all, you were twins. Her dark eyes, hair and the way she smiled. You both have such an infectious smile and that same dimple when you laugh. I did have to listen closely to hear what she was saying. Her hoarse voice had something to do with that goiter growth in her neck."

"Russ, take your mother and dad into the parlor where they will be more comfortable. You kids stay here and help me clear the table and rinse the dishes." Mother stood up and motioned for Dad to leave the table. Dad wiped his mouth on the linen napkin and escorted our grandparents into the parlor. Les and I helped Mother put the leftovers away. We rinsed and stacked the dirty dishes for later. I knew I would be stuck with washing the dishes but I didn't mind when Grand-pap was around. I wanted him to be proud of me and continue to take me fishing. I hated to see Grand-pap and

Grandma prepare to leave after pumpkin pie. Dad wrapped up some turkey and trimmings for them to take home. Grand-pap bent down and hugged me as always. He never realized how tight he hugged me, so tight it always took my breath away.

I watched through the window as Grand-pap steered his new green 1948 four door Chevy away from the curb. I thought about prior Thanksgivings. Many times we traveled through unplowed roads, but always to Grand-pap's we went. When we arrived, there was the smell of turkey from the old cook stove in the kitchen. Grandma was always in the kitchen feeding in kindling to keep the fire going and watched as she raised up slowly supporting her back. When up straight, she stood just short of five feet wearing a flowered silk jersey dress with a freshly ironed apron pinned to the front. Her silk stockings were rolled to ankle length above her black oxford shoes. She wore a baking hat with a few white wisps of hair slightly visible from the side.

Everyone gathered in the kitchen with their contributions of home baked goodies. Also, the kitchen was the warmest room in the farm house. The freshly baked pumpkin, apple, and raisin pies were lined up on the kitchen cabinet. And, always Aunt Dot's chocolate cake beside Grandma's raisin applesauce cake that no one could ever duplicate.

Ring-a-ling. A loud buzz follows. I'm startled! Oh, damn it's the alarm. Tick tock, it's 7:00 o'clock. I turn off the alarm. A vigorous rub of my eyes and I realize I had been dreaming. I lay back and try hard to go back to sleep. No luck! Now I remember what day it is. It's the day before Thanksgiving. No wonder I dreamed about my Grand-pap.

Reality sets in. I have chores to do, pies to bake and a thawed out turkey breast to roast. That is, if I want to have any resemblance to Thanksgiving for myself. More importantly, I promised my neighbor a pumpkin pie. She will have guests. But, there will be no family, friends, hugs, laughter or fun for me. It will be just another routine day like every other day for the past ten months.

I slowly drag out of bed following my terrier dog, Daisy, with her tail wagging. Why did this have to be the worst pandemic since the 1900's? A few moments ago, I was with my family at Grand-pap's. I awoke from a dream that was so vivid with my dear parents, grand-parents, aunts, uncles now gone. It's no wonder why I try to go back to sleep. My dreams aren't as frequent these days. But, when I do dream it's refreshingly real. I'm thankful for the escape they provide.

My day to day existence during this COVID-19 virus running rampant has been routine with nothing out of the ordinary. Each day a replica of the one gone before it. When I dream of the old days among family and friends, it's the best part of my day. Then I relive the wonder of them as I relay them over the phone to others. It's a blessing. I'm able to remember their content after awakening. I'm thankful for Daisy, her companionship and my dreams as I walk about my neighborhood. But, I've had enough! I want to travel again, see what family I have left unmasked, face to face, and hug them close up. When I no longer have to keep my mandated distance. However, my dreams of the past visiting family will have to continue to sustain me. Meanwhile, I will continue to share the memories and happy times, just dreamed, with anyone who will listen.

CAT'S IN THE CRADLE
WILLIAM JOHN ROSTRON

When my mom passed away a few years ago at almost 96 years of age, my sisters and I had the task of emptying a life's worth of belongings from her apartment. The chore of sorting through almost a century of memories was gut-wrenching enough, and emotions were raw. It was then that a particular song started to play on the radio.

A child arrived the other day,
He came into the world the usual way.

Memories about relationships began to flood my brain—those between my parents and me, as well as my relationships with my children. At the forefront of my thoughts were the stark emotions created by Harry Chapin's memorable, "Cat's in the Cradle" song. This classic song describes a father who fails to bond with his son because he is too busy. His commitments to work and almost everything else took priority over quality time with his son. Yet, the son in this tale continues to ask his father to do things with him, only to have the father reject him. However, he holds out hope that the situation will change and responds,

I'm gonna be like him,
You know I'm gonna be like him.

That could have been my parents, but it wasn't. Even as my

mother grew to need increasingly more and more of our time in her nineties, we gave it to her. This was not because of any sense of obligation but rather because we wanted to. We had learned to give of ourselves from both my mother and father.

Ironically, as the song still played in the background, I came upon yellowed copies of every article I had published in the last forty years. She had placed them in a box after showing them to her friends. I am glad that I made her proud because she was the one who always insisted that I get an education, even if it meant that she and my father had to work multiple jobs to help me to do so. It meant a great deal to her that I fulfilled my dreams because she had not been able to. My mom had wanted to be a teacher, but the Depression had deprived her of that. However, she became our teacher, always having time when needed. When my sisters and I were grown and had families of our own, she continued to make time for all of us. And still, that was not enough.

Until the age of 86, she continued to work at a local college library. She helped students do their research in pursuit of the degrees that I know she valued so highly. When our entire family tried to dissuade her from working, her answer was simple, "I don't need to do this. I do this because I enjoy being there with the kids and helping." She had hit upon the definition of a teacher, thus fulfilling her lifelong dream. I would not be singing "Cat's in the Cradle" for her.

My father did not even graduate high school. Instead, he chose to join the navy at age 17, eventually rising to the level of Chief Petty Officer. Because he had been in the navy before, during, and after the war, he had a golden opportunity for advancement. However, it would have meant months at sea away from his family and a deleterious effect on his children.

"When you coming home, Dad?" (The Son)
"I don't know when, but we'll have a good time then." (The Father)

Instead, my dad took a job that wasn't exciting, well-paying, or prestigious. However, it allowed him to be my baseball coach, take me swimming, and enjoy all those nights when we watched TV together and laughed.

And even more importantly, he taught me the power of reading. Despite his lack of formal education, he always had a book in his possession. When I was young and enamored with the newly popular phenomena known as TV, he would always insist that it should not replace the habit of reading. Even with no formal education, he taught me, a smug, know-it-all preteen, about the power of the written word. With time and patience, he got through to me. I grew up not only reading incessantly but also spending three decades teaching reading and writing.

> *"Can you teach me to throw,"* (The Son)
> *"Not today, I got a lot to do,"* (The Father)
> *"That's okay."* (The Son)

No "Cat's in the Cradle" for my dad either. He somehow had time for catch even after working two backbreaking jobs. And when he got home too late to spend a sunny afternoon at the beach, the whole family would instead sit at dusk around a campfire at the shore, laughing and telling stories well into the night.

Somehow, my two parents had known how to do it right. We never had money, but we always had each other and a good time until the very end of their lives.

As the song ended, I had a slight smile on my face recalling that my mother had died surrounded by four generations of our family, and every single one of them *wanted* to be there instead of being *obligated* to be there. However, I felt sad for the father *in the song*. In the end, his lifelong behavior of not being there for his son resulted in that son not having time for him when he became an adult. He indeed had become like his father.

> *"I'm gonna be like you, Dad,*
> *You know I'm gonna be like you."*

So why was this song such an emotional minefield for me now? Why was it so engraved in the fabric of my being? I jokingly always tell anyone who will listen that my Baby Boomer generation should have been called the "Sandwich Generation." With our parents living well into ages thought impossible before modern medicine made it so, we had both the pleasure and the responsibility of seeing them through their advanced years. When my parents were younger, Social Security was created, and the age set for collecting was 62. There was a reason for this—that was the average lifespan in the 1930s. By the turn of the 21st century, that lifespan had become almost 80. I laugh at the number because the last members of my family to pass away were aged 95, 96, 99, and 106. They were the top of my Baby Boomer sandwich. The bottom slice of that sandwich is our children.

Many of those turning to adults in the 1950s and 1960s left home by their early 20s. However, for economic and social reasons, most of the generations raised in the 1970s, 1980s, and 1990s stayed in the nest longer, married later, and started careers later. That may be a good thing. However, it often resulted in their dependency on their parents for an extended period. That created the bottom of the sandwich, with the Baby Boomers as the lunch meat in the middle. I don't compare myself to bologna often, but it seems to fit. And it doesn't bother me. However, in my case, I wanted that sandwich to be perfect. I wanted the bottom to be just as good as the top. I wanted to be as good a parent as I had had. So, that brings me back full circle to the "Cat's in the Cradle" song."

Harry Chapin wrote the song in 1974, and it became the number one hit on the charts in December of that year—exactly three months before our first child was born. I don't think that my wife and I were alone in the fact that we obsessed over what kind of parents we would be. Would we make all the right moves? Would we be firm, yet tender enough with our children? Would we give them the tools to succeed or help them find their way to happiness?

And would we make mistakes? Okay, over time, you realize that all parents make mistakes. The key is to learn from them and try not to make them recurring ones. Yet, listening to that very same song on the eve of the birth of our first child stirred the hearts and minds of us very young parents. I knew every verse, and throughout our three children's youth, I would find myself murmuring the words "cat's in the cradle" to myself when I needed to decide about priorities. Do I go to his game or go out with my friends? Cat's in the Cradle. But to be honest, I enjoyed the ride. I wouldn't give up any of the more than two decades of cheering for the kids in sports, listening to their concerts, or camping with them. And yes, even reading them stories about little boy blue and silver spoons.

The cat's in the Cradle,
And the silver spoon,
little boy blue and the man in the moon.

I won't tell you it was easy. We offered our children a full life, and they took it: sports, music lessons, and extended family vacations. I realized just how much of a commitment we were making on a specific day in 1988. My wife and I looked at our religiously organized calendar of obligations. In that month, our three children (13, 11, and 7) were scheduled to play for eleven different teams and take three sets of musical lessons weekly. My wife and I had to decide if it was too much—were we spreading ourselves *and them* too thin? We realized that we might be wrong if *we* decided what activities to cut. We might force them to quit something that they thought important. However, soon each child would eventually pick their path and follow it, and the array of events would somehow be whittled down to only the most vital.

I remember driving one of my sons to a game that was more than an hour away. After a rough soccer match, the drive home found him sound asleep in the passenger seat. It was then that *the* song came on, and I started to sing along. He woke up from his nap and immediately asked, "What's a cat's cradle?" Thinking I would pass on one of life's lessons, I relayed what the song was about. He looked at me like I was crazy and went back to sleep. However, he must have heard at least some of what I said because he relayed the story to his mother, brother, and sister at dinner that night.

A child arrived just the other day,
He came to the world in the usual way.

My children are grown now, in their thirties and forties, and have children of their own. We recently all got together to enjoy a holiday. Eventually, the first cousins started to play by themselves, and adults relaxed around the table. I noticed a calendar hanging on the wall just teeming with scheduled events; swim meets, piano lessons, Taekwondo classes, and so much more. Meanwhile, the conversation turned to the upcoming week with my other two children discussing the forthcoming volleyball game against a traditional rival and the guitar lessons, acting lessons, and more that they all had to attend.

My wife and I sat back and smiled quietly, reliving our own experiences of being stretched too thin.

Finally, after holding in my amusement for a while, I half-jokingly remarked, "I don't know how you all do it!"

However, I don't think they knew I was being sarcastic and all three of my children turned to me at once. They smiled at each other. Their expression betrayed the fact that some sort of conversation or conversations on this matter had occurred at some time in the past. Perhaps many times in the past. I watched the interplay of their eyes as it became evident that I was right in my assumption. I could see them give a discreet nod to each other, saying, *It's time.* A time to reveal a long-held belief. They held up their glasses, clinked them in a toast to my wife and me, and said in unison, "Mom and Dad, we learned well—"Cat's in the Cradle, Cat's in the Cradle."

HOW I FOUND MY SIXTH
COUSIN TWICE REMOVED
DONALD ECKERLE

My mom's mother was born in France. That was my mission, to find where in France. I remember my mom saying that grandma spoke both French and German. Unfortunately, grandma died when mom was only 3 years old so she didn't remember too much about her. Mom was the 4th of her 5 children so she heard stories about her mom from her older siblings. Grandma's death certificate didn't tell me anything, but a translation (from French) of her marriage record from the Church of St. Louis indicated that she was born in Lorraine, France and gave me the names of her parents.

My older siblings remembered that she had a brother who had lived in Port Jervis, NY and were able to tell me a few stories about him. So, I headed to Port Jervis and obtained his death certificate. At the library in Port Jervis, I found his obituary on the microfilmed local paper. His obituary said he was born in "Mombron, Alcase-Loraine, France."

When I returned home, I went to the Family History Center and searched the Catalog of films in Utah. In the catalog, I found that there was a microfilm for the records from Montbronn, Moselle, Loraine, France. I ordered it and waited anxiously for it to arrive. When the film arrived, I was stunned to see that it contained copies of Family Group Sheets, in English. WOW, this certainly will make it a lot easier for me. I found grandma, her siblings, and her ancestors back 5 generations. There was a note at the beginning of the microfilm, from the person who created the Family Group Sheets, giving the LDS permission to microfilm her records. The note also contained a phone number of the person. I decided to call her and thank her for doing this.

I called. A man answered. I told him who I was and that I wanted to thank June for her work on the records. When June came to the phone she said, "Who the heck are you?"

I explained that I was using her Family Group Sheets. She said, "Why are you interested in those records?" Let me also mention here that her tone was anything but friendly. It was almost nasty. I then told her that I was interested because my grandmother was born in Montbronn and these records have helped me to get back a few more generations. "Your grandmother was born in Montbronn?" Yes she was, I replied. That's when her tone changed and she said "Then you and I are cousins. Now what you need is a copy of everything I have." WOW!! I gave her what info I knew about grandma. About 2 weeks later I received a copy of all the family group sheets, a book from Montbronn and a note that said 'You are my sixth cousin, twice removed."

June and I keep in touch. We talk on the phone every few months. She lived in Idaho. As it turns out we were in the same Catskill resort at the same time many years ago and her grandmother lived only a few blocks away from me in Queens County. What are the odds.

SAFE HOME
DIANE KANE

There are the names we are given and others that we earn.

Matilda Harris was born on September 7, 1924, in Belfast, Northern Ireland. She hated the name Matilda. Her family in Ireland called her Wee Tilly. But in 1949, when she crossed the Atlantic Ocean on a big ship to America, her life changed, as did her name. After some time, she became Ma, Aunt Tilly, Nana, and eventually Great Nana, all names she earned. But there was more to Tilly than just a name. She touched many lives. Some she touched rather firmly with the straw end of a broom. Although Tilly was not inclined to soft sentiments, her love was true. Tilly never said goodbye; instead, she wished her family and friends 'safe home,' and there were never two more meaningful words.

Family shapes us like a lump of clay in the hands of an inexperienced potter.

So it was for Tilly. Born the third child of Thomas and Ellen Harris, her Da worked as a trolley car driver on the streets of Belfast. Her Ma was the queen of their home off the Shankill Road. Tilly had one brother Bobby, who sang Ole Danny Boy with the passion only an Irishman can. Her three sisters, Lilly, Susan, and Sara shared Tilly's genes but not her fierce spirit.

Ellen's brother Sandy was born with a bad leg and never married.

Uncle Sandy became the nanny, cook, and housekeeper. He was also the resident loan shark, always obliged to lend a coin with a wee bit of interest. He took his earnings and shuffled to the pub. Tilly and her sisters would retrieve him, locking arms like drunken sailors on the stagger home.

The price for fashion was paid with sweat in the early 1940s.

Tilly finished the eighth grade and began working in the shirt factory at fourteen years old. She worked all day to buy the latest style of dresses and shoes. At night she went to the theater in Belfast and watched American movies. Her friends swooned at the likes of Carey Grant and Clark Gable. Tilly admired Katherine Hepburn. When she got older and the Navy ships came into port, Tilly and her girlfriends danced with the Yanks. Irish brogue mixed with Yankee accent and made the world seem smaller.

Sometimes the shoes you walked in were not always your own.

Her father's job on the trolley afforded the family a little cottage called the Wren's Nest by the sea on Isle Magee. Tilly and her sisters spent every weekend there in the summer with friends. They traveled for hours after work on Friday, first on their father's streetcar, then aboard the train and transferred to a bus. They walked the final muddy mile to the small cottage perched on the rocks. At night, they crossed the field to the barn dances. They paused in the moonlight at the local farmhouses to borrow rubber Wellie boots sitting on farm porches while carrying their dance shoes so as not to get them dirty. At the end of the night, they made their way back across the field and returned the Wellies safely to their homes—leaving the farm women to wonder the next morning about a little extra mud and the perfume of fairies on their boots.

The war came early to Belfast.

The winds of war blew into Belfast on September 3, 1939. Harland & Wolff shipyard produced warships, making Belfast a high-value target for German bombers. Windows were blackened, and lights were forbidden after dark. Food and clothes were rationed. Thomas Harris cleaned out the coal closet and placed eight stools inside. The family sometimes huddled for hours in the dark, waiting for the all-clear siren to sound. One night the bombers kept coming, and everyone was ordered to go to the shelter. Thomas Harris declined and sent his family to the closet. He peeked out the window before joining them and saw the white parachuted bombs floating toward the shelter.

Meanwhile, Tilly volunteered as neighborhood air raid warden. She kept her water bucket full to grab and run out into the night, extinguishing small fires caused by flaming shards of falling metal. A helmet was required for the job, but it didn't deter Tilly from doing her hair. She twisted her long locks in wet rags each night before bed to put a wave in her straight auburn hair. When the siren sounded, Tilly jumped from her bed. She pushed her helmet on, grabbed the waiting bucket, and ran out the door with rags streaming from under her metal headgear.

A letter of excitement.

When the war ended, a letter came from Uncle John, Ellen's brother in the United States. He and her brother Robert had immigrated to America several years earlier. Robert married late in life, but John remained a bachelor. John wrote to ask if one of the girls would like to come to see America. He didn't mention any strings attached. Tilly being the oldest at home was given the first choice. Her father didn't want her to go, but Tilly arranged to get a Visa and shots.

On June 25, 1949, Thomas Harris brought his daughter to Liverpool, where she boarded the HMS Nova Scotia with her first-class ticket that Uncle John had sent. Tilly traveled across the Atlantic, stopping in St. John, Newfoundland, and Halifax, Nova Scotia, where she had her first ice-cream soda. Sixteen days after leaving, Tilly arrived in Boston, where she found that America wasn't as glamorous as the movies she had seen on Ireland's big screen.

Broken dreams.

Uncle John's live-in housekeeper, Dinah, had been with him for many years. She ruled the roost almost as if she owned the place. When Dinah was in her 80's, Uncle John anticipated needing a replacement. His plan was for Tilly to be his new housekeeper. But Dinah wasn't ready to give it up yet, and she did everything in her power to make Tilly want to leave. She cut up Tilly's clothes and destroyed letters from home before Tilly saw them. Dinah prepared Tilly cold, tasteless food and forbade her from the formal living room. To top it off, Tilly was forced to sleep in a room with a large portrait of Dinah peering down at her.

Finally, Tilly ran away to a cousin in New Jersey. But she couldn't bear to shame her father, and eventually, guilt forced her to return. Her cousin dropped her off at Uncle John's house, and Tilly knocked on the door with drooping shoulders. She stood on the doorstep for hours in the cold until Dinah let her in without a word.

Love sometimes walks in at the most in inopportune moments.

Tilly got a job at Abbott Worster Mills within walking distance in the village of Forge in Westford, Massachusetts. She planned to save her money for passage back to Ireland. After a year, Tilly had saved the money to return home. But it wasn't meant to be.

Tillie walked to her Uncle Robert and Aunt Annie's house in the Village. A young man came by while Tilly was taking her lunch there. "Ahh, don't fret; it's only Cookie, my sister Margret's boy," Annie dismissed. Lawrence (Cookie) Kane served in the Army as a Seabee during the 1940s. Cookie came by his nickname as a cook in the military, and the name stuck. He returned to the village to work as a carpenter and inadvertently fell in love with Tilly.

In May of 1950, Tilly started dating Cookie, and in August, he asked her to marry him. Cookie gave her a solitaire diamond ring for her birthday on September 7, 1950, and they were officially engaged. Tilly feared writing for her father's consent to marry. It wasn't her age that was a factor; Tilly was twenty-six—it was religion. Thomas Harris was a proud protestant and a member of the Orangemen in Belfast. Cookie was an Irish Catholic. In Ireland, it meant war, and in America, the two did not mix well either. Cookie's father, Lawrence Sr., thought Tilly would take his son from the Catholic church. Tilly didn't see how it could work, but she agreed to write to her father and ask permission. Tilly and Cookie waited months for the letter to cross the Atlantic and for the answer to make its way back.

Tilly gave up. She had enough money saved, and she told Cookie that she was going home to Ireland. Then the letter arrived. Thomas Harris said if his daughter truly loved Cookie Kane, she had his permission to marry him. Thomas needn't have spoken a word of the union in Belfast, but honor compelled him to resign from the Orangemen in disgrace. In December of 1950, at the age of 26, she became Tilly Kane. She took her vows in Saint Catherine's Church outside the altar railing and signed a paper stating that her children would be raised Catholic. Uncle John gave her away. Dinah wept with tears of joy and even gave Tilly a gift of money.

A house is built, a home is born.

In 1951 Tilly apprehensively accompanied Cookie to the bank to ask for a loan for $5,000. She feared being able to pay their mortgage payments of $39.00 a month. Cookie built a home with his own two hands on Forge Village Road in Groton, Massachusetts. Tilly told Cookie she wanted eight children; she had nine. In January of 1952, Linda was born, and Tilly became Ma. Over the next twenty years, Peter, Thomas, Susan, Larry, Timmy, Kathleen (Number 7), and John made eight. In June of 1971, at almost forty-six, she gave birth to Lisa. They all grew up in the four-bedroom cape with one bathroom that Cookie built. Timmy and John followed in their father's footsteps and became carpenters.

There was little time or money for photos.

If pictures told the story, Tilly only had two children, her oldest Linda and youngest, Lisa. Number 7, Kathleen never let her forget. Cameras were not a top priority, but family was. Tilly's love was not always loud, yet it was strong. In public, she defended her children with the heart of a warrior. Privately Tilly didn't hesitate to give any of them a *bloody dig in the bake* when necessary.

Home is where ocean meets the rocks on a different shore.

In 1954 when Tilly told Cookie she was homesick, he packed up the station wagon with the kids and brought them to the coast of Maine. She gazed upon the rocky shores and said it looked like home, or at least close enough. Tilly's youngest sister Sara had come from Ireland to live in the village with her husband and raise three boys. Tilly and Sara saved their pennies each year for one week in Maine with all the children. Tilly never drove, so they all squeezed in Sara's car and made the two-hour trip to Maine. They rented a run-down two-room cottage, dubbed the Sugar Shack. The roof leaked, and the plumping was spotty at best. Tilly and Sara sat on the beach like they didn't have a care in the world. Tommy spent all his saved-up money the first day, and all the children ran unsupervised in the small beachside town. They all survived.

Some things are lost while other things are found.

In 1964 Cookie lost his job and a little of his pride. Tilly did what she had to do. Cookie never took to Tilly working nights at Murray Printing in the bindery. By the time Cookie got another job, Tilly had embraced her newfound freedom. When Cookie finally found work again, Tilly refused to quit her job. Cookie never forgave her. Linda became the second mother of the house. They all watched over Cookie the best they could.

Heartbreak knows no boundaries.

In July of 1977, Tilly made a long overdue trip home to Ireland. It was a time of religious unrest in Belfast. Businesses were draped in barbed wire, with soldiers checking for weapons at the doors. It was here that Tilly got word that Cookie had died of a heart attack at fifty years old. It took her several days to book flights to get back to America. At fifty-two years old, Tilly was a widow with nine children, her youngest five years old. Tilly had her night job at the bindery and managed to make ends meet. The older children mothered the younger ones. There was no other choice. Tilly retired in 1989, the year Lisa, her youngest, graduated high school.

In 1990, Tilly returned home to Ireland again. The barbwire was gone, and there was a peaceful reprieve in the streets of Belfast. Tilly visited her sister Lily when word came that her oldest son Peter was in the hospital dying. Peter had tested HIV positive at a time when it wasn't spoken about. When Peter could hide it no longer, it was too late. His brothers and sister took turns staying with him in the hospital night and day. Tilly hurried back from Ireland in time to hold Peter's hand. It was all she could do. He passed away at thirty-six years old.

Home is where the heart is, or so they say.

Tilly sold the family home to Number 7, her daughter Kathleen in 1997. She moved into a spacious apartment over her daughter Lisa's garage. She decorated with lighthouse decor and read without interruption. When the family gathered at the family home for the holidays, Tilly held the babies with a tenderness she never afforded her own. Her wish was to be a great-grandmother before she died. She had sixteen grandchildren and four great-grandchildren.

The long road home is not for the faint of heart.

At eighty-seven, Tilly was diagnosed with blood cancer. She

came home to the room and the bed she shared for so many years with Cookie in the house he built. For two weeks, the house was filled with Irish memories, music, and love. Everyone gathered to hear the stories again, to sing the songs, and to say goodbye. Tilly smiled when she reminisced about Dinah. She hoped that she was headed in the opposite direction, and they wouldn't meet again.

On the evening Tilly passed away, her sister Sara and her son Larry sang to her, "We'll Meet Again Some Sunny Day," in not-so-perfect harmony. Sara kissed her sister goodnight. Tilly took her last breath and went home. What she left behind was more than a name.

Safe home, Tilly, safe home.

THE LOST COUSINS AND THE CEMETERY CRISIS

JANET METZ WALTER

NOTE

My daughter attended several genealogy seminars through an organization she belonged to about 15 years ago. Knowing that I had a lot of notes from my parents about my relatives and family history, she invited my husband and me to attend one of them.

I have a cousin who was considered the family historian, but I decided to do my own family history chart for my children and grandchildren, especially since my daughter now seemed interested. Yes, it was a chart, not a tree. I found it easier to write and easier to read, but rather than just a chart, I also included notes about family members, their jobs and other things I remembered about them.

The first chart was of my father's family, and they got interested in seeing it, so I sent it to them. It backfired on me, as people took issue that I talked more about one person than another, one cousin had heard the story differently than another and so on. I decided that when I did my mother's side of the family, that it would only be a chart.

I had more of a job to do with my mother's family. My generation of cousins that I had grown up with had gotten lost through the years. I was hesitant to deal with it again, but then I got an interesting phone call from a cousin who had grown up on the west coast, whom I had only met once or twice. Another cousin that I did keep in touch with occasionally, who was doing a family tree, gave her my number.

She wanted to know if I knew anything about her grandfather and his second wife. I informed her that he was not biologically related to me, her grandmother was, he had died before I was born, and I had no information about him. She seemed confused about who I was and my relationship to her, so I decided it was time to put together the chart of my grandmother's family. Now that I am writing this story, it should be noted that what I say is from my own experiences, along with the stories I was told, and is totally from my own perspective. Other family members will have different memories and a different perspective. I have already discussed this fact with certain family members. Most of them were still happy to receive the chart and fully cooperative about giving me information.

This story is about more than a chart. It is about losing touch with family and finding them again, and about how a family came forward to help me in a time of crisis. I have changed names to protect people's privacy, and have modified a few facts not affecting the story for the same reason.

My parents were the cousin keepers. They each kept in touch with all the cousins they knew growing up, and my brother and I knew and saw all of our local cousins, my mother's first cousins and their children, and even the ones who lived far away. As time passed, and times changed, people became more mobile and while the first generation of cousins kept in touch, the second generation went away to college, moved around the country and in most cases, lost touch with each other.

My great grandparents, Aron and Ruth, were married in Breslitov Russia and decided to emigrate to the US in 1890 or 91. After doing research on Ancestry.com, and city records, I was unable to find the city they left from, or the ship they arrived on.

I also found out the censuses in those days tended to be grossly inaccurate. People changed their names, lied about their age or birth date, or the census takers just did not spell names correctly. My grandmother was one of six children, but one did not live past childhood. That left three boys and two girls.

They lived in an apartment on the Lower East Side, a few blocks from the building that is now the Tenement Museum. Great Grandpa Aron's occupation was listed as Watchmaker. By the 1900 census, the last name had already changed several times, and birthdates differed greatly. In 1900 Ruth was listed as age 41. In 1910, her age was 57. She aged pretty quickly. Most of the children were listed in 1910 as being only 7 or 8 years older than they were in 1900, which was actually probably more accurate, since in later years when I was doing my research and taking their ages off their gravestones, they were all two to three years younger on the gravestones than on the first census.

My grandmother Doris is listed with an incorrect spelling on the 1900 census, and her age was listed as 11. By 1910, she had lost two years and was listed as age 19, which would make her birth year 1891. Depending on what month the family arrived in New York, she could have either been born in Russia, or even on the boat, but she always insisted that she was born here in the US, so we chose to believe her. In my personal records, I have her birthdate listed as Nov 1892, and that is what appears on her gravestone.

The third name was what stuck until the boys were in their 20's. It is a very common name in the Jewish community, and I believe Great Grandpa Aron felt that they were assimilating into the community, however as the boys went for jobs and found a certain amount of prejudice, they each changed their name yet again to a more indefinable name.

The family eventually made their way to The Bronx. Grandma Doris married Grandpa Daniel in Oct of 1917, and my mother Selma was born in the beginning of 1919. Her brother Arnie was born at the end of 1920. He was learning disabled, possibly due to an unfortunate accident while my grandmother was pregnant with him. Fortunately, he was not physically handicapped, and was able to function up to his own abilities.

No one ever talked much about Uncle Arnie's friends or playmates. I really do not know much about their early childhood, except that they grew up surrounded by cousins on both sides of the family.

Each of Grandma's three brothers had two children. Mom kept in touch with all of them, but her best friend was Bev, who had lost a sister and became like a sister to Mom. Then there was Emma, Grandma's older sister. It is her family that forms the center of this story. Emma married Jake in 1910. His family owned a very successful clothing manufacturing company. They had four children, three sons, and one daughter.

Jake was quite wealthy, and he soon moved his family to a large house in Queens. The house was in a quiet middle class neighborhood a block away from a busy main road, but hidden behind a large beautiful church. They had an acre of land with a formal garden in the back. A fountain graced the middle and beautiful Hydrangeas, and other plants and flowers, benches and trellises were scattered around the garden. Life, however, was not all flowers and beauty. In the 1930's Jake decided to divorce Aunt Emma and move to California with the love of his life. He left Aunt Emma the house and enough money to live on. As each child grew to college age, they were brought out to California to attend college.

As the children left, Aunt Emma, who of course in those days was mortified and furious to have been abandoned, decided that she wasn't giving up the house and the life she had made for herself in the neighborhood. As the older and bossier sister, she decided to implore Grandma and Grandpa to give up their apartment in the Bronx and come live with her.

Grandma was 7 years younger, and had a more passive and compliant personality. They decided that the move might be better for Mom and Uncle Arnie, even though they were leaving a lot of family behind.

Shortly after Mom graduated from college in 1939, they packed all of their possessions in barrels and moved to Queens. From that day on, they never had their own home. They lived in Aunt Emma's house. The barrels went into the basement. Cousin Lloyd, the youngest, may have still been in the house for a while.The census showed that there were two other women who had lived in the house. One may have been a nanny, one may have been a relative or renter, but by 1939, they were gone.

There was a Nanny's room off of Lloyd's bedroom that was assigned to Uncle Arnie. There was a bed, dresser and wardrobe set up in the attic and that became Mom's abode.

Sometime in the late 30's, Grandma's three brothers decided to invest in a family cemetery plot in a Jewish cemetery on the Queens/ Brooklyn border. They bought a plot of 16 graves and designated them for their families, and for their sisters and their spouses. Uncle Henry's daughter Elaine was the first to be buried there in 1938, followed by her father Henry in 1944 at age 61 and his brother Jack in 1946 at age 59. It was not that uncommon for men to pass that young in those days.

Aunt Emma, although she was on the family plot, decided to buy the plot of 8 graves that was next to the family plot and designated the graves for her four children and their spouses.

World War II heated up in the early 40's and the young men were drafted to serve. Even Uncle Arnie was called to duty. At that time, they did not do the same type of ability testing as they do today.

When it was discovered that Uncle Arnie had learning disabilities, he was sent off to France to ride around the battlefield in a truck, picking up the bodies of those who were killed in battle. He also rode around in a tank, handing ammunition to other soldiers. He claimed he knocked on doors making sure people were OK. This could have meant anything.

Meanwhile, Aunt Emma was not alone in her degraded status as a divorcee in the 40's. She became friendly with a younger woman named Tillie whose parents, Rivka and Wolfe, were also divorced.

Wolfe was one of the premier portrait photographers in Brooklyn, especially wedding portraits. He eventually remarried and his wife got the benefit of his thriving business, while Rivka did not.

Tillie introduced Emma to Rivka. Rivka lived in an apartment and was not as well off as Emma, but they had things in common. She had five children including a set of twins, Izzy and Lev, who were also in the army.

Tillie, Aunt Emma and Grandma Doris played Mah Jongg together, and they decided it would be a great idea to introduce Tillie's brother Lev to Selma. Selma and Lev met each other and got married not long before Captain Lev was discharged from the army.

I was born 18 months later, and my brother Matt was born a little more than 3 1/2 years later.

Aunt Emma's two sons came home from the Army also. One became a doctor and settled in California. The other, Bert, had brought home an English/Irish war bride. He was a traveling salesman. They had five children in five different states and finally also settled in California. I was acquainted with his children because when they were young, they came to visit Aunt Emma once or twice a year. She visited them in California once or twice a year, and spent time in Las Vegas also. Once they moved to California, I had no contact with them at all. Aunt Emma turned out to be quite the gambler. In those days, the machines did not have push buttons, only the arm that you pulled down to spin the slots. She would literally come home with her hands bandaged when she got blisters from the hours spent pulling the machines.

Meanwhile, Uncle Arnie also got married to a woman named Ruby. Her mother immediately moved in with them. Uncle Arnie's hobby was photography. He got a job printing up posters for Rheingold Beer. His favorite part of the year was when Rheingold sponsored the Miss Rheingold contest. He got to meet all of the candidates and print up the posters that were hung in stores and subways featuring all the contestants. Despite what he went through in Europe, he was a pleasant, friendly man, but very simple.

While he was busy working in Brooklyn, his wife was working at entertaining other men in her Long Island home with the full knowledge and consent of her mother. They never had children and after about 10 years of marriage, they got a divorce and Uncle Arnie left the house and moved back into Aunt Emma's house with Grandma and Grandpa.

On weekends he became the chauffeur and errand boy, but he also pursued his photography, went to local dances and social groups and found other women to date.

It also meant that my brother and I had no first cousins on my mother's side of the family. Mom remained close with Aunt Emma's daughter Edith. She got married and moved to New Jersey. Her husband traveled a lot for his job. For several summers when he was away, Dad would drive us there for a weekend and go home again.

Edith had three children, a daughter and twin sons. We usually had fun there. I saw my first Disney movie with them, *Lady and the Tramp*.

One time my leg got caught in a post hole on the property when we were playing outside. I had to be rescued.

One time, Dad came to pick us up and he and Mom were folding away the sleeper couch and they trapped the cat in it. Fortunately the cat survived. She jumped out before they actually gave the final push.

Several years later, when I was already engaged, Edith's husband got a job transfer to Germany. They were there for several years, then moved to Colorado. Two of the kids eventually moved to California. We kept in touch very sporadically.

Aunt Emma's children made it pretty clear to her that they were not going to be buried in a cemetery in Queens NY.

Mom and Dad told Aunt Emma that they would like to buy two graves from her, and she made arrangements to have them deeded over to them. She also put in her will that one grave would be reserved for Uncle Arnie.

Mom remained close with her New York cousins. She talked to her cousins in Westchester every few months. Bev and her husband moved to Queens not far away from my parents. Mom talked to her several times a week. Bev and Mom really were more like sisters. A few years later, they moved to a house on Long Island. They had two children, a daughter and a son. Aunt Emma's son, Lloyd, and his wife also lived on Long Island, a few towns away from Bev. His wife started a dress boutique in her basement and when the people in town got to know her, she opened up a store in town. Bev and Mom used to shop there occasionally and visit with her. They had 3 daughters. Alisa, the middle daughter, and Matt became closer as they grew up.

I met my husband Ken in the mid 60's, and we got married after he served a two year stint in the army. When we were married three months, Grandpa Dan had a heart attack. We went to visit him in the hospital. When we arrived there, we found out that he had passed away from kidney failure. Now Grandma and Uncle Arnie had to figure out life with Aunt Emma. When our son was born in 1975, Bev was named as his godmother.

Aunt Emma passed away that same year. She was 90 and had outlived not only her brothers, but some of her nieces and nephews. That's when life changed.

Her family on Long Island had moved to Florida.

Several years before her death, Aunt Emma had sold the land in back of the house to a developer who built three houses on the property. Some of the property was sold to the church who built a school there.

Aunt Emma left the house and all of her possessions to her daughter Edith. The will stated that she had left a grave to Uncle Arnie. There was nothing else left to anyone in our family, or as far as we could tell to her sons, although we only had a few pages of the will in our possession, the ones that dealt with Uncle Arnie. There was an affidavit from her son Bert in California that he was giving up his rights to his grave and giving it to Uncle Arnie. It was pretty clear that Uncle Arnie had a spot in the cemetery.

Not unexpectedly, her children wanted to sell the house, and told Grandma and Uncle Arnie that they had to move out as soon as possible. With Mom's help, they found a garden apartment in a development not far from Mom and Dad.

Mom was on a Macrobiotic diet and she and her friend Betty went to meetings and distributed newsletters to stores. She convinced Uncle Arnie that he should be in on it too. He joined the club and helped them distribute the newsletters. He went to a senior citizens club in the neighborhood. I think he was happier there than he had ever been at Aunt Emma's house. Grandma passed away in 1978, when my daughter Donna was 4 months old. Now Uncle Arnie was on his own for the first time in his life.

Mom kept tabs on him, especially since he was now helping her with her newsletter deliveries.

Bev's mother passed away in 1979. That was the year my brother Matt got married to his wife Jessica.

Bev developed Breast Cancer, which was misdiagnosed, and she was gone 4 years later in 1983. She was 57 years old. It was a shocking and terrible loss to the whole family. Matt and Jessica had their first child Darren the same year. Somehow or other, the births and deaths in the family seemed to coincide. One life ended as a new life was beginning. The pattern continued. Matt and Jessica's second child Alicia was born in April of 1986. Sometime around June, Mom developed non alcoholic liver cirrhosis. Mom had had several conditions during her life, including thyroid problems, major allergies to foods and medications and some other issues. She had been a Biology major in college and thought she could handle all of her issues through diet, acupuncture and other means. They did not work. She passed away in August on Darren's third birthday, only three years after Bev. She was 67. Now it was Dad's turn to look after Uncle Arnie. That didn't last too long. Dad reconnected with a childhood friend who was also widowed and they were married 11 months after Mom passed. Dad moved to Florida with his new wife. He passed away on her birthday in 1992.

Meanwhile, although Uncle Arnie seemed to be doing fine on his own, it fell to me and Matt to keep in touch with him and help him out. We didn't know what we were in for.

Uncle Arnie had retired and had started a business by circumstance. The older ladies in the neighborhood that he had gotten to know through the senior center started offering to pay him to drive them to the doctor, supermarket, cemetery, wherever they needed to go. It gave him something to do and he was happy to do it. They paid him for his gas, and usually gave him a little something extra for the favor. This lasted several years. Then he got into an accident. He wasn't badly hurt but the car was totaled. We decided that he needed to stop driving. He was in his eighties, and no one was getting him a new car.

Periodically we went to his house and looked over his checkbook to make sure he was paying his bills. He was paying more than his bills. There were checks every month to Publisher's Clearing House. He was sure that the more he paid, the better chance he had of winning.

He wrote checks to anyone who solicited him - Madam Zalonga the Fortune Teller, Health Magazine, The Fire Department, any organization that asked for a donation. There was one check made out to cash for thousands of dollars. He could not or would not tell us what happened to the money.

Matt and I were frustrated but unless we took over his life, we did not have much control over what he did. He seemed pretty OK otherwise, although his mental acumen seemed to be declining a bit.

We also noticed that every time we picked him up to go to a relative or a doctor, he was waiting for us outside. He said he didn't want us to have to get out of the car to ring the bell. On a July day in 2009 Mom's friend Betty called me. She had gotten a call from Uncle Arnie that his air conditioner was not working. It was 102 degrees. She told me we had better go over there. It happened to be a Saturday, so we went over there. He didn't want to open the door. We told him he couldn't stay there in this heat if the AC was out, and we had to look at it. When he opened the door, we almost fell over. You couldn't even walk into the room. It was as if someone had spilled a dumpster full of trash into his house. We asked him what was going on. He said he didn't know. It had gotten away from him. He had become a hoarder and couldn't throw anything out.

Fortunately, we did not see any food trash. It was all mail, envelopes he had opened but not thrown away. Mail and papers and newspapers filled the entire apartment, with bags from stores and wrappings from packages and even some clothing.

There was a daybed in the living room that usually folded into a couch that had a sheet, a cotton blanket and a pillow with an undershirt as a pillow case. We asked him if that's where he slept. He said yes, the other bed was Grandma's. Grandma had been dead for 30 years. His clothes and other personal possessions were in the bedroom. We had no idea that he did not sleep in the bed there. Now we knew why he always waited for us outside. He seemed to know that there was something wrong that we should not see.

He took me into the bedroom and showed me his checkbook and bills. At least it looked like he was paying them.

We took Uncle Arnie to our house and called Matt and told him we were calling in a junk removal company.

The junk removal guys came on Monday. Ken was on vacation so he went over there. I was at work.

Ken helped the guys drive over 100 bags of garbage to the garbage room around the corner. The following weekend, Matt came over with his wife and son to look through the closets and drawers. They found mouse droppings in one closet along with a blanket that Uncle Arnie had evidently had an accident on.

It became obvious that Uncle Arnie needed help. Matt and I had to do a lot of research to figure out Uncle Arnie's eligibility for a Home Health Aide. We were able to get help for 6 hours a day. It wasn't long before we realized it wasn't enough. We started looking for Assisted Living facilities. It wasn't an easy task. We eventually got him settled in a lovely facility that had a lot of activities. Unfortunately, they did not take Medicare. We got him his VA assistance and he was OK for the moment. He liked it, and settled in pretty quickly. It was Sept of 2011.

Meanwhile, we decided that we would do a funeral pre plan for him so we would have less to do whenever it was that it was needed. Everything was kind of sticky because we were not Uncle Arnie's children, but we were his next of kin. Everyone else was gone.

The cemetery was totally obnoxious. Even though it was clear in Aunt Emma's will that he had a grave, and they had the papers from her son Bert renouncing his grave, the cemetery maintained that if a grave number was not assigned to him, they needed all of Aunt Emma's heirs to sign off on it.

Matt figured out that since Aunt Emma had left everything to Edith, and Edith had passed away several years before, that her heirs were the ones who could sign off on the grave. Fortunately, out of all the cousins in California, it was Edith's children that we happened to be in touch with.

I contacted them and they agreed to sign off on the grave.

We sent them affidavits to sign. They gave me their brother's address in Colorado to send him one too.

They all signed. The cemetery office said that they weren't notarized, and they still needed all the other heirs, but they would keep these on file. We had no idea where any of the other heirs were.

Ancestry.com was booming. Everyone was spitting into bottles and suddenly finding a tree full of relatives. It was 2015 when I got the call from my cousin Jane, Aunt Emma's son Arthur's daughter, about her grandfather.

Edith's son was already building a family tree, but he was missing a lot of information about his grandmother's family. He knew that I knew all of the cousins that he didn't. Because they had grown up on the East Coast, he had heard some of the names from his mother, but he needed more information. He was the one who suggested to Jane to call me. I knew who my cousins were, but I had no idea about their spouses and children and where they all were. Even though they were second cousins, being Aunt Emma's grandchildren, they were the closest thing I had to first cousins, but I had lost track of most of them.

Jane gave me some information about herself and her siblings. It was like crocheting a chain stitch by stitch.

I contacted Edith's daughter, and she gave me information about herself and her family. The bonus was that she told me that she kept in touch with Alisa in Wisconsin, and she gave me her email.

I wrote an email to Alisa and she answered me immediately. A phone call followed. I knew her sister Julie had passed away because a gravestone had suddenly appeared in the cemetery, but no one seemed to know anything about it. Alisa gave me her information and that of her sisters. Her parents were the only ones who had still kept possession of their two graves, which was why Julie was there.

I eventually also spoke to her sister Michelle, who was still living in Florida. Another stitch in the chain.

Then Alisa informed me that she was Facebook friends with her cousin Connie, the second of Bert's 5 children. She gave me her email address. Another email went out. Connie told me that her parents were gone. I had known about Bert, he passed away the same year as my mother.

Two of her siblings had passed away under tragic circumstances. She also told me that the person I really should talk to was her brother Jack.

Jack was three months younger than I and had more contacts and more worldly experience than she did. The chain was linking. I had not seen or heard from any of these cousins in over 40 years.

I sent an email to Jack. Much to my surprise, Jack asked if he could call me. Of course, I was thrilled. Jack and I connected like turning on a light. He remembered playing with me at his grandmother's house when we were 10 or 11 years old. He remembered some of the relatives. We spent over an hour on the phone catching up with the missing 40 years and promised to keep in touch. After that we spoke every few weeks.

———————

The next step was finding the cousins from Grandma's other siblings. Matt and Jessica were in touch periodically with Mom's youngest cousins because they lived close to each other. We knew where to find Bev's children.

The next big surprise was when I googled a cousin who had lived in a mansion in Westchester. I found her in California. She was a writer. She brought home the fact that what you see on the outside is not always the way it is inside the home. When their mother had passed away, their father had remarried and life took a nosedive. She went to California, her brother was living in Oregon and the other sister was still in New York.

The cousin in California gave me her brother's email, and both of them were very willing to get involved in the project. I asked him for the number of his cousins, the sons of his mother's sister, the only ones I had really never met, even though I knew and had been very fond of their mother.

He contacted them and told me that they had no interest in the project, so he just gave me what information he knew. I now basically had my information for the document. About a year later, his sister came to New York and met me for lunch. We had a lovely afternoon walking the High Line and catching up on each other's lives.

It had been between 40 and 50 years since I had seen most of these cousins, and suddenly I had them back again, and they were interested in keeping the links to me connected. The East Coast and the West Coast had never had very strong links, but I was the link to all of them. It was kind of mind blowing. Some of them found out about others for the first time when they received the family chart. Their parents were not as good as mine were about relatives.

We had held on to Uncle Arnie's apartment for about a year, but once we knew that he was OK in assisted living, we put the apartment up for sale. The money was to be used for his living expenses. By the time I was in touch with the cousins, he had been moved to the Memory Care Unit. He had had a good four years.

We realized that money was running low. We were going to have to move him to a less expensive facility.

We were sad to leave this place that had been so good to him and for him, but we had no choice. We found another place, but we were not happy with it.

Although I had not heard great things about VA hospitals and nursing homes, Matt found out that there was a fairly new one in Stony Brook that was supposed to be very good. We put our name on the list. It just happened that a friend of mine had some connections there and was able to get him in. I was sorry that I had been so stubborn about it, because it was so much nicer than the other place. It was September of 2016. He declined rapidly. He had had a cold that did not seem to go away. He passed away at the end of November, just about a week before his 96th birthday. This simple minded guy who lived a simple life that became complicated for us, had outlived everybody in his generation.

We called the funeral home and they called the cemetery. They called to inform us that the cemetery would not accept him for burial because every heir of Aunt Emma had not signed off on his burial.

We informed them that they had papers from Edith's heirs. They said that they had not been notarized and that they wanted them all. Part of the reason could have been that they saw dollar signs. They wanted $37.50 for each affidavit for each heir. We couldn't believe our ears. Every child of Aunt Emma was dead and buried elsewhere. There were five graves in the plot that would be empty forever. No second cousin in California was coming here to be buried, but the people in the office stood their ground. There was a grave but no specific grave dedicated to him. Now that I actually knew where all the heirs were, I emailed all of the cousins related to Aunt Emma and each one said of course they would sign papers. From California, to Colorado, to Wisconsin, to Florida, everybody was ready to cooperate.

Matt decided to take matters into his own hands and spoke to an attorney. When the attorney wrote a letter to the cemetery office, they were furious at Matt because there was not supposed to be any legal action involved, but now that there was, the office finally backed down and allowed the burial.

I finally happily told the cousins that the matter had been settled. They all remembered Uncle Arnie from their childhood. After all, he lived with their grandmother. They all sent condolences. Some of them did not get along with each other. Some had other problems, but they all came forward to do the right thing for me and Matt and Uncle Arnie, and for this I thank them profusely.

EPILOGUE

Matt had been very close with Alisa at one time. She moved from Wisconsin to North Carolina to be close to her grandchildren, and he and Jessica had a lovely visit with her and her family when they stopped while on their vacation in the area just before the Pandemic.

In 2017, a friend of mine invited me to go to California with her to meet her son and his friend who were coming in from studying abroad to renew their visas. I decided to go. I called Jack to ask if he might be available for dinner one night. My friends were going to San Diego, and he lived in Orange County.

He did me one better. He asked if I could come to his house and stay over for the two days that they were going to be in San Diego. I was shocked that he asked when in effect he hadn't even met me as an adult. He said he just knew that it would be fine.

It was more than fine. It was a wonderful two days. His wife Penelope was a lovely hostess and the three of us formed a wonderful bond. We talk to each other every few months. It was good timing. We might not all have bonded this easily when we were younger, we all lived totally different lives, but we are all happy to be cousins again now.

SURPRISE REUNION
JASMINE TRITTEN

The forty-minute flight from Athens to the Greek island of Kos, near the Turkish border, seemed endless. I sat next to my travel friend Mark, squirming in my seat, and glanced out the window with butterflies in my stomach.

Mark leaned over and offered me a piece of gum. "Here's something to calm your nerves before meeting your mother."

With shaky fingers, I removed the wrapping and popped the chewy substance into my mouth. After a while, I relaxed. Below us, the crimson sun slowly descended into the cobalt blue ocean. Soon the sky darkened, and we arrived at the small airfield.

My insides quivered thinking about being with mother again. She had controlled me for the first twenty-one years of my life in Denmark until I immigrated to the United States of America for adventure. Seven years had passed since I last visited her and the family near Copenhagen. We had corresponded for years, but I had a need to see her again to repair our rifts from the past. We lived on opposite sides of the earth from each other which seemed okay for a while, but I felt compelled to connect with her again. Maybe she would stop criticizing and telling me what to do.

Mother had no idea I planned to meet her on Kos, but she knew I had been traveling in Europe and Egypt with a friend. In one of her sporadic letters, she mentioned a ten-day trip to Kos with our family friend Grethe and included the dates. *What a fantastic opportunity!*

"Why don't we surprise my mother in Kos, since we are here in

Greece? Maybe I can repair my relationship with her," I suggested to Mark.

"That sounds like a good plan. I would love to meet her after everything you have told me about her," he said. *This is about as good an answer as I can get from him. Hurrah!*

At the time, iPhones and computers did not exist. We had to be creative getting to the island of Kos. After locating a travel agency in Athens, we found one airplane flying to Kos the day before mother arrived.

Thoughts swirled in my mind. *I wonder how Mom will react to Mark. He is my friend, travel companion and bodyguard, but not a serious prospect for a long-term relationship. I hope she will understand.*

Upon arrival at the Kos airport, Mark and I grabbed our luggage. In my handbag, I carried *Frommer's Greece Guidebook.* I located and called the highly recommended Hara Hotel and asked for a room. A lady with a strong Greek accent answered the call. "Yes, I have one room available if you like."

By the time we finished the conversation and thanked her, the terminal had emptied of passengers. Outside, no taxis. One loaded bus drove off before we got a chance to inquire. A minute later, two cleaning ladies appeared.

"When is the next bus to Kos?" I asked.

"The last one leaves at ten o'clock." They answered simultaneously in pidgin English. *That's a long wait in such a desolated place.* With a sigh, I lowered my head. My shoulders slumped.

As Mark and I sat down on a wooden bench and waited, the air chilled. All the lights dimmed in the airport buildings, then went out completely. Darkness surrounded us. My heart jumped into my throat, and I grabbed hold of Marks' arm.

"I wonder if the bus will ever arrive, or we'll have to sit here until the morning?" I shivered through my whole body.

"Don't worry, we'll get there." Mark put his arm around my shoulders.

Tomorrow, tomorrow, how is it all going to turn out? My chest tightened. *I can't even imagine how I will feel the moment I see my mother.*

Finally, out of nowhere, the headlights of a bus shined in our direction and illuminated part of the sky.

"Hurrah," I yelled and jumped from the bench. Only Mark and I waited for the bus. A small person with a tan cap crowning his head let us on the motor coach together with our luggage. Without a word he nodded. Obviously, he spoke no English and acted tired.

For half an hour, we rode in dead silence. When I looked out the windows, the sky appeared pitch black. In my mind I visualized a lush green landscape. At the end of the trip, the driver gave us directions to the hotel using finger language. *It feels eerie arriving late at night in a strange place. So glad I am traveling with my friend and bodyguard.*

Mark knocked on the front door of the hotel. Finally, a distinguished-looking gentleman opened the door and bowed his head, welcoming us. His wife Hara, owner of the hotel, came out and introduced him.

"This is my husband, Nikolas. He's a criminal investigator for government affairs in the Greek Islands, except he is on vacation now," she said and looked at him.

Up and down my spine I felt goosebumps but tried not to show any reaction. *She might scare us deliberately by telling us about his profession.* Her slick black hair was pulled back from her round face and tied in a bun. With piercing mahogany brown eyes, she eyeballed us and said,

"You both can stay here as long as you want, but you are the only guests in our small hotel."

At first, we hesitated. Then I whispered to Mark, "I am not crazy about us being the only ones here, but what else are we to do so late at night?" Mark nodded in agreement. So, we stayed.

"Let me show you the best room with a view of the ocean." Hara led us up a spiral staircase. *There is nothing to see at this time of night.* She handed me one key, for both our room and the hotel.

"If you need anything or have any problems, I live next door," she said.

A pleasant smell came from the cedar furniture in our room, which added a certain charm to the place. I opened the balcony doors, leaned back my head, took in a couple of deep breaths of fresh ocean air, and sighed with relief. Then I crashed on my bed and slept like a dead horse.

The following morning, I stepped outside on the small furnished balcony and glanced across the deep blue water to the mountains of Turkey. Thoughts of surprising mother circled in my mind. The morning sun warmed my shoulders, and I turned to Mark.

"All this beauty for only 1,000 Drachmas =12 Dollars a day. That's a bargain." Across my face a smile began to spread from one side to the other thinking of the upcoming reunion with mother.

For breakfast, we sat down and consumed the sweet, sticky baklavas from the day before and washed them down with bottled water. Then down the stairs we flew and rushed next door, to Hara, the owner of our hotel.

"Please tell us when the Charter flight arrives from Copenhagen today, and where is Hotel Atlantis? I plan to surprise my mother." I bounced on my feet in anticipation.

First, she gave me a map of the island, marked the location of the hotel and how to get there. Then she opened her black book. "The plane is scheduled to arrive at 3:30 in the afternoon." My heart pounded in my chest. *Just enough time to prepare for our surprise.*

"Let's go to Hotel Atlantis now," I suggested to Mark. "Here's the map." I handed him the directions.

Palm trees swayed in the wind as we walked through a park. We passed the ruins of a fortress, the harbor, and strolled along the shore, where waves sparkled in the sunshine. A whiff of the salty sea tickled my nose. About thirty-five minutes later, a glorious white building appeared on the sandy beach. We entered Hotel Atlantis.

"Yes! Your mother is on the list to arrive this afternoon," the concierge confirmed. I sighed in relief. *Only a five minutes' walk to dive into the ocean from here. An abundance of sunshine. What more could Mom want? Except for me?*

On the way back towards our hotel, we walked through the charming old town of Kos. Smells of donkeys, goats, sheep, and turkeys filled my nostrils. Three stray dogs followed us for a while. We carefully examined the architecture of the ancient light-colored buildings, influenced by Turks and Italians. At the center of town, Mosque *Lotzias* glowed in the sun. Next to the harbor, we spotted the Kos Museum and the massive Crusader fort constructed by the Knights of St. John about 1315 AD.

As I lay down to rest at hotel Hara, my belly ached, and I could hardly breathe. Negative thoughts swirled through my head. *What if mother is not coming? They could arrive late. It's possible she might be upset with me because of my divorce two years ago. She might not accept me bringing Mark. Or maybe she wants to be alone with her friend Grethe.*

The time came for us to return to Hotel Atlantis and surprise my mother when she arrived. My whole body trembled. In my suitcase, I brought a huge "Welcome to Kos" poster for mother I had created in Athens using white cardboard with green and red markers.

"Let me carry the sign," Mark offered. He placed it under his arm.

"Flowers! I must have flowers for Mom," I said in a loud voice. "Let's stop on the way through town."

I selected pink and magenta blooms, exuding beauty, and love. The friendly staff at Hotel Atlantis gave me a key to my mother's room. They suggested we go there in advance to wait for her arrival. For the flowers, the concierge brought a glass vase.

Mark placed the enormous sign on the bureau. Next to it, he put a small box with the gold ankh, a symbol of eternal life, I had purchased for my mother in Cairo. Outside, on her balcony, we sat down to wait in wicker chairs. My stomach churned. I clutched my hands.

Suddenly, the phone rang in the room. I rushed over and picked up the receiver. "Your mother and her friend have arrived," the bellhop alerted me. I hurried back outside to hide. Two minutes later, we heard the door open to the room. Somebody walked in. Immediately, I detected mother's distinct Danish accent in her high-pitched voice.

"Oh, what is this?" She must have seen the sign and box. We heard her say, "Oh, Jette has sent this to me. How sweet of her." Jette was my name at birth.

Outside we sat and chuckled, attempting to stay quiet. We heard footsteps get closer. Then we saw my mom walk through the open balcony doors. She stared at the ocean, looked around, and then spotted us.

"I don't believe this." With arms outstretched, she rushed over to embrace me and burst into tears. We hugged and hugged for the longest time. Teardrops streaked our cheeks. Birds took flight at the sound of our laughter. More hugs and then we danced around nonstop for an eternity. At the end of the commotion, Mom looked up and spotted Mark.

"And who is this young man?" She pointed at him.

"My good friend Mark. We are traveling together," I explained. He walked over and embraced my mother. My mouth fell open.

Moments later, Mom's friend Grethe, pushed through the door to the room carrying her luggage. As soon as she noticed me, she dropped everything, and her face lit up. She ran towards me. More hugs and tears.

"What is this? What are you doing here?" She yelled in her usual loud voice.

"I'm surprising Mom."

For moments we all stared at each other in disbelief without saying anything. The thrill was mutual. From her travel bag, Grethe pulled out a bottle of Ouzo she had bought in the duty-free shop at the airport and left-over crackers from the flight. For hours we sat on the balcony mesmerized gazing at the ocean, talking and celebrating.

The surprise meeting and quality time spent together on the charming island of Kos became a tremendous healing experience and repaired the relationship between my mother and me. The last fifteen years of her life, I called mother every day from America. Each time, we talked for about half an hour, always ending with laughter.

My mother lived to be 101 years with a mind clear as a bell. No dementia. I was with her when she died in Denmark. I am so grateful we reconnected in Greece. Of course, I loved my mother. Our reunion showed me she loved me too. As we both aged, we became closer than ever living oceans apart. So glad I had the courage to surprise her with a reunion of a lifetime.

THE JOURNEY OF A LIFETIME
RENÉE TONE

Growing up, I always knew I was adopted. My adoptive parents told me when I was five and starting kindergarten. There was a book they read to me and the usual, very careful reassurance that I was "special," "chosen." In fact, I was told that my very existence had made that of my younger sister possible, as my mom had battled infertility for fourteen years before adopting me. As happens so often, once I came into the picture, she relaxed, and when I was thirteen months old, she became pregnant.

Being adopted was something I was quite pleased about as a very little girl. I'm told it was my proud Show and Tell offering one day at school.

All in all, I had a happy and uneventful, rather idyllic childhood, a real Norman Rockwell tableau in which kids played in each other's backyards until dark fell, went bike riding all over the neighborhood, built snow forts in the street in front of our houses and went sledding in the hills behind the elementary school. There was summer camp every July and August, Brownies and Girl Scouts, sleepovers with friends, art and dance lessons, secret clubs, and the carnival we kids on the block put on one summer as a charity fundraiser, in the lush back garden of old Mr. Nagel, who lived in the palatial house on the corner.

As for what I knew about my actual origins, there was the story I'd been told from the very beginning, added to gradually over the years but still not quite complete. I was half Jewish (mother's

side) and half Italian (father's side). My mother's family were
Orthodox and connected somehow with the garment industry in
New York City. Both my parents were just eighteen and unable to
care for a baby. As the story went, my father proposed to my mother,
but she turned him down. There was a certain nobility to doing that,
I always felt. She must surely have recognized that her family would
never accept him, and that the proposal was not being made out of
real love anyway, but because it was the honorable thing to do.
Knowing this, she chose the harder path and refused.

The adoption, a "gray market" transaction, was handled
privately by an attorney who had originally found a different baby for
my adoptive parents. That deal had fallen through when the baby's
mother changed her mind. Then the attorney learned that I was on
the way, and a new deal was struck. My mother was shipped off to
Florida to wait out her pregnancy in secret, her expenses paid by my
adoptive parents.

I surprised everyone by arriving early and subsequently spent
time in an incubator. According to the narrative, my adoptive parents
were at a Broadway performance of "The King and I" when they
were contacted with the news that I'd been born. My adoptive mom
hopped on a plane down to Florida, where she waited to take me
back to New York. When I was finally ready to be released from the
hospital, so the story went, she stopped on the way to buy diapers
and formula for the trip back to New York. When she arrived, my
mother was holding me. Handing me over, she said, "Take her now,
before I change my mind." This was the poignant conclusion of the
story of my origins as I'd always known it. The narrative informed
my sense of myself for many years: I'd come from a brave, self-sacri-
ficing eighteen-year-old girl, nobly doing the right thing and relin-
quishing her tiny newborn, never to lay eyes on her again, and that
baby on the cusp of a whole new life in a stable, comfortable, secure
family setting.

Adoptees are often told that they should appreciate having
been adopted, that they should be grateful. The assumption, particularly during the "Baby Scoop Era" (mid-1940s to the early 1970s),
was that of course, the adoptive family had so much more to offer a
child than a young, single mother with no money to speak of, no

training, and no means of support, either financial or emotional. So often, families with a daughter who became pregnant out of wedlock kicked her out to fend for herself or banished her for the duration of her pregnancy to some distant place where she wasn't known, forbidding her to come home with a baby in tow, because of the perceived shame she'd brought on them. Either way, young, pregnant girls were given virtually no choice about how to handle their situation. They had to stay silent and go along with the lies. Society frowned severely on illegitimate children, and, far from finding ways to support unwed mothers, adoption as an industry was born and thrived, benefitting countless doctors, lawyers, and social workers.

I knew nothing about any of that. I bought into the myth. And although, in fact, I was very fortunate in the adoptive parents I did have, thoughts of my mother came and went, especially around my birthday, when I would wonder, year after year, if she remembered me and whether she ever thought about me, especially on that day. Over the years, I asked questions, but all answers were exhausted eventually. I hit a wall, beyond which I could not go. Somehow, I had to be content with the narrative as I knew it. It seemed there was no way to break through and learn anything else.

Then, one day when I was in college, I happened to be at home and had a sudden urge to see if I could find my adoption papers. My dad kept all important records in a metal box on the floor of his bedroom closet. My parents weren't home; I had the house to myself. So, I sat down on the floor of his closet and opened the box. It didn't take long to locate the file with my name on it. I can still remember, all these years later, the way my heart pounded as I opened the file and began to examine the papers inside. Three items practically leapt into my hands: documents from the surrogate court that had finalized my adoption at the age of six months, a typed note to my adoptive parents from the attorney, and a slip of lined paper with a handwritten surname penciled in at the top and physical descriptions of both of my parents: height, weight, hair color, and jobs. I learned that my mother, an office clerk, had been a petite five feet, two inches and 120 pounds, with light brown hair. My father, a dress presser, had been tall and lean at six feet and 160 pounds, with dark brown hair. The name scrawled above was "Krimsky." I decided that must have been my mother's surname. It sounded Jewish.

However, the biggest shock came when I examined my adoption papers. Scanning the pages, I discovered that I'd begun life with another name altogether, one that had been legally mine until I was six months old. I was stunned. Here was another piece of me I hadn't known existed, and now I was meeting that part of myself for the first time. Somewhere in the world, there was a woman, now in her late thirties or early forties, who'd given birth to a dark-haired baby girl twenty years earlier and had given her a beautiful name.

"Curti," my legal surname originally, was surely my father's, I concluded. It sounded Italian. I took that file folder – it was rightfully mine, after all, now that I was over eighteen – and tucked it away, mulling over the new information, paltry though it was.

Over a decade passed and I was now married with small children of my own. I'd learned of an organization called ALMA (the Adoptees Liberty Movement Association), and now I went so far as to fill out an application to join, but I stopped short of pursuing an active search and all that it would involve. My children were very young, and I couldn't be away from them; moreover, a search would be very costly and time-consuming, neither of which I could afford. All of that was true. But deep down, I knew there was a far more powerful reason: I was scared. Scared of rejection. Every adoptee knows this fear. It gnaws relentlessly at your confidence and your sense of self-worth. What if I actually managed to find my mother and she didn't want to be found? I didn't think I could handle that. So, I did nothing.

Decades passed. My children were now grown, one daughter newly married. I remember waking up on the morning of my birthday with a question I could no longer ignore: was I really going to go through the rest of my life never knowing anything about my parentage? Most importantly, were my parents still alive? They'd be in their early eighties by now. Further, did I have half-siblings out there in the world that I knew nothing about? Nieces and nephews? Cousins? Maybe my parents were already gone and I'd missed my chance. But I knew that I had to try. Now that DNA testing was both accessible and relatively inexpensive, maybe I could find the answers

to these questions at last, despite the fact that New York, like virtually all the rest of the country, was a closed-adoption state, the
records sealed, and would remain closed for another four years. With
great excitement, I ordered a DNA test from Ancestry.com, spat into
the small plastic vial, dropped my sample off at the post office, and
waited. I felt like I was on the edge of a precipice. Knowing that I
would finally learn something concrete about myself, maybe even
connect with close family members, was exhilarating and a bit scary
at the same time.

While I waited, I made sure to submit my personal information to every adoptee site available: for starters, the New York State
Adoption and Medical Information Registry, ALMA, and the
International Soundex Reunion Registry (ISRR). I received my "non-
ID" record from New York State, but disappointingly, there was
virtually no information about either birth parent beyond the most
rudimentary references to age and profession, all of which turned out
to be untrue in any case. No information about physical appearance,
family health history, religion, or personal interests. My mother had
done a very good job of covering her tracks.

The wait from Ancestry can be absolutely excruciating,
anywhere from a quick three weeks to longer than eight. It feels like
an eternity as you eagerly track the progress of your saliva sample on
a chart on Ancestry's website, the icon inching along from "Kit Acti-
vated" to "Sample Received," and finally, to the all-important and
thrilling "Results Ready."

At last, my results were posted on my Ancestry account. My
heart was in my throat as I examined the information. My ethnicity
breakdown was true to what I'd been told. No surprises there. What
was intriguing were the cousins, three in all, with whom I'd been
matched.

One had a distinctly Jewish surname, so I put her in my
"maternal" column. The other two didn't give anything away in
terms of their surnames, but neither was connected by DNA to the
obviously Jewish relative, so I concluded for the time being that they
were paternal cousins. Further digging would later reveal that both
of them shared the same Italian surname in their family backgrounds,
starting with the letter C.

Painstakingly, I began to build two very detailed family trees on Ancestry, starting with the two pieces of information I felt I could trust: the surnames "Krimsky" and "Curti." Both trees had names, histories, dates, and records, such as Social Security information, US Census records, birth indexes, voting records, ships' manifests, phone book listings, marriage and divorce registries, and school yearbook photos. I was positive I had the right families, since so many details fell neatly into line with what I'd been told all my life about my biological parents and their backgrounds. More to the point, I was pretty sure I knew the identities of my mother and father. Critically, the surnames and ages according to the narrative's timeline were exactly right. In the latter's case, it appeared that he could have been one of two brothers; the other was already deceased. I would have to contact the surviving brother and take it from there. It all felt very right. I sat down one evening to take the next steps: direct contact.

As any adoptee will affirm, taking those next steps is terrifying. Questions flood your mind: do I try to reach them by phone? Or do I compose a letter and hope desperately that it's received – and that there is an actual response? What if they hang up on me? What if my letters are ignored?

Eventually, I had a three-page letter, describing myself and asking if the information was at all familiar, if there had been a pregnancy in the family years before that had ended in a private adoption. I enclosed photos of myself as a baby, a little girl, and a young adult, as well as a current picture.

I sent one fat envelope off to an address in Brooklyn, NY, and the other one to an address in New Hampshire. And then I waited. But it wasn't enough. I would have to reach out another way as well. With my heart in my throat, I summoned the courage to make a phone call to the woman I was certain would turn out to be my mother.

Nerve-racking as it was to make a cold call, I was half-relieved when I got the answering machine instead of a live human. I left a message and crossed my fingers.

Days passed and there was nothing, either in the mail or by phone. My letters had required a signature, but nothing came back to me, until one day, when the letter to my presumptive father showed up in my mailbox, stamped "Person Unknown" or words to that effect. The letter to my "mother" never came back, and neither did the proof of receipt.

While waiting for those responses, I had discovered a possible relative with the right paternal surname actually living in my neighborhood. She very graciously met with me and did a DNA test too. She should have shown up as a first cousin, but in fact, the result was negative. We were not related. All leads had dried up. And now I was forced to conclude that the name "Curti" was most likely a made-up name, a red herring. The paternal family tree I had so meticulously constructed was completely wrong. To say that I was surprised and disappointed would be an understatement. But I also felt even more determined to get to the bottom of the Brooklyn situation, at least. I decided to drive there in order to scope out the house and the surrounding neighborhood of Victorian Flatbush. In a strange, roundabout way, it felt like doing that, at least, would bring me closer to my mother, somehow. At least I would be doing *something*.

That weekend, my husband, older daughter, and I drove to Brooklyn, parked the car near to the listed address, and walked up and down the block, looking to spot neighbors I could talk to. At that point, I just wanted to know if anyone knew her, had seen her around the neighborhood, just anything at all that might fill in some blanks. One person out walking his dog said that he did know her, but that he hadn't seen her in quite some time. Not an encouraging sign.

Then my daughter said, "Mom, why don't you just knock on the door?"

Instant wave of panic. The thought of doing such a brazen thing turned my knees to water. "Oh God! What on earth would I *say* to her?" I asked. "'Hi, I think you may be my mother'? Seriously?"

The idea seemed absolutely ridiculous. Nevertheless, I found myself standing at her front door and knocking, still not quite believing what I was about to do.

A tiny woman with dark hair opened the door. "Can I help you?"

"Hello. My name is Renée Tone. I'm an adoptee, and I have reason to believe that we might be closely related."

"How?"

I paused, gathering myself. "I believe... you may be my mother."

I will never forget the stunned expression on the woman's face. She stared at me blankly, utterly bewildered, and finally got one word out. "Why?"

Now my words came tumbling out in a rush. I explained that I'd written to her but hadn't heard back, and I pulled out my copy of the letter and photos I'd sent to show her. I told her about the painstaking research I'd done on Ancestry that had led me to the likelihood that she was my mother. She remembered the phone message I'd left, believing it had been a crank call or a scam. It's a very common reaction adoptees encounter when trying to make contact with a potential or known birth relative.

So many factors had lined up, and even she had to acknowledge that. At last, though, she smiled wistfully, shook her head, and said, "I wish I were your mother. You seem like a lovely person. But I'm not." Then she went on to explain why, despite all the boxes that had seemed to be ticked correctly, it couldn't be true.

We talked for quite a while about our families and our lives. Her relationship with one of her own daughters was rocky at best. As I was leaving, she said she would have loved to have me as a daughter instead. This struck me as particularly sad, coming from an 83-year-old woman who, at this point in her life, should be enjoying her grown daughter instead of being estranged.

Now I had to accept that the maternal tree I'd built so carefully was totally wrong as well. All that work for nothing! I was frustrated, but at the same time, I knew that the chance of hitting the right mark on the very first try was a million to one. Back to the drawing board.

Over the next two years, I followed one trail after another. There were a lot of red herrings. Reaching out to the known paternal cousins, I heard nothing from the one in Virginia, and likewise, nothing from the one in New York. However, I did make contact with the second/third cousin on my maternal side; we actually met and spent time in front of her computer, looking at all the information I'd already gathered about that side of the family. She was very excited to meet me and to see what I'd found in old documents during the course of my search. From her, I learned quite a lot about one branch of my maternal side. That family surname was N–, my great-grandmother's married name. Logically, one of my grandparents would have had the same last name. On the other hand, the surname "Krimsky" remained a frustratingly unyielding enigma, and I stopped pursuing it actively.

Building a new paternal tree, I researched the C name that had emerged in the hunt for details about those two cousin matches. I hit some very frustrating stone walls in the process, one of which was the sheer number of immigrants who had arrived from Italy in the same year, with exactly the same names and very similar birthdates. I wondered how on earth I would ever know which one was the right one! There had to be a way of narrowing the search down and eliminating some of the many duplicates. Here's where having a good search angel, an individual who assists adoptees in their search, can make a big difference. I had an excellent one. While I did the majority of the research myself, it was great to have someone to whom I could put questions, who understood the complexities of DNA relationships and could help me assess the significance of the information I was uncovering. As I said, there were a lot of dead ends, but there was some bizarrely dark comedy too. At one point, I was rather horrified to learn that I might be related to a gangster who'd done time. A daughter I contacted was able to refute that idea. It was a relief to remove that character from my family tree!

A lot of other leads ended up fizzling as well. I asked another potential first cousin on the maternal side to take a DNA test, which I provided. It ended up going nowhere, much like the rest of that search thread. On the paternal side, however, my focus had narrowed to one family in particular. There were three brothers, all close in age, any one of whom could have been my father. All three were now deceased. One of them was the father of the cousin to whom I'd already reached out. She had never bothered to answer. Another was the grandfather of the other cousin I'd tried to contact, also to no avail. The third one had two sons, and I wrote to both of them. Neither one answered. Summoning my courage again, I cold-called the one whose phone number I had found. I held my breath while his wife called him to the phone. Yes, he remembered my letter, which he admitted he'd simply shoved into a drawer and forgotten. But he wasn't at all thrilled with the idea of taking a DNA test, fearful that somehow, the government would get hold of his personal information and use it in some nefarious way. I reassured him that he could use an alias and also that his test results could always be destroyed if he so chose. I just wanted to know if he and I were half-siblings. Then I'd have the confirmation I needed to prove the identity of my father. At last, he relented, and I ordered the test. He received it in good time, and I began eagerly watching my Ancestry account (his test was in my name, managed by me) to follow the progress of his test, once his sample had been received.

The wait turned into weeks, far longer than it should have taken. I called again, hoping he wouldn't simply hang up on me and cut contact forever. He admitted he'd sat on the test instead of sending it back, unsure of what he wanted to do. I reminded him that Ancestry would destroy his results if he wished. There would be no record. At last, he agreed. After that, things moved pretty quickly. His sample was received and processed, and before too long, the results were in: he and I shared 1,788 centimorgans of DNA. Confirmed half-siblings!

Things were moving quickly for another paternal thread as well. And here's where amazing coincidences can play a role. My older daughter was scrolling through Facebook one day, looking for the other cousin with whom I'd been matched, and found her brother instead. Incredibly, it turned out that he and his wife had gone to college with my younger daughter, and all of them had a friend in common. This was exciting news, because it was another way in, a way past the natural resistance and suspicion that adoptees so often encounter during their searches. My younger daughter reached out to the mutual friend, who then contacted this cousin on my behalf and asked if he would be willing to talk to me and fill in some family details.

He was, so I emailed him immediately. He answered right away, but said that his mother would be a far better source of information and that he'd forwarded my email to her. Before long, I heard back from the woman who would turn out to be my first cousin and with whom I have since become good friends.

She was able to add to my knowledge of the family significantly. Names, dates, and places could now be added to the tree. Questions were answered. Best of all, she turned out to be really nice. We arranged to meet, and coincidentally, it turned out to be on the same three-day weekend that my half-brother had planned a trip to my area. He and I arranged to meet for lunch one day, my cousin and I two days later.

Those afternoons were pretty intense. In both cases, we sat for hours, talking. With my half-brother, I asked a lot of questions about our father: what was he like as a man and as a dad, what was life with him like, what were his interests and talents, what was his temperament like, and then the basic things everyone wants to know about: health history and related issues. We covered a lot of ground in three hours. I asked if I looked like our father, and my brother said yes. I had always suspected as much. I got an earful about what sort of father he'd been, ending with "You're lucky you weren't raised by him," the depressing final thought my brother left me with as we were leaving. It hadn't been information I'd hoped to receive, but it was what it was. At least I knew his identity now, and I saw a few photos of him in middle age and as an elderly man.

Two days later, my cousin and I met, and it was a very different experience. The moment we said hello and hugged, there was an immediate connection. It was eerie and very gratifying to see how alike we looked, too. That's something adoptees keenly miss: looking like family members. Because of course, the resemblance marks you as a part of the clan. You feel connected, that you belong. It's hard to grow up without that powerful connection. You feel rootless. I always felt as if I'd been dropped from the sky from who knew where, with no idea who had given me life and who the people were that I'd come from. In fact, of course, I was never meant to know. I was merely supposed to understand that "it was all for the best," that "you're special because you were chosen," and finally, the pièce de résistance: "your mother loved you so much that she gave you away." Nice words for a small child, but such sentiments wear very thin for an adult who has spent a lifetime yearning for information, roots, and true closure.

My cousin had brought a family photo album with her, and we pored over it together after lunch. Altogether, it was a wonderful day, and the start to forging a genuine connection with several cousins, for me and for my children as well.

Time passed. I was still deeply invested in the search. Truth to tell, as important as finding my father was, finding my mother was even more critical. There is something deeply compelling, even sacred, about a mother-child connection. There cannot be a closer one. It's beyond the capacity of mere language to describe adequately. You carry a growing child inside your body for nearly a year. You nurture and protect that developing new life. That tiny baby is with you every moment, waking and sleeping. It feels your heart beating and hears your voice. Gradually, it makes its presence known. You talk to the baby, sing to him or her, tell stories. And when he or she finally makes an appearance, the bond is immediate as you look into each other's eyes and feel the warmth of skin-to-skin touch. Because I'd been premature, my mother had likely missed out on that crucial first contact, assuming that the hospital even permitted such contact for mothers of babies slated for adoption. Most hospitals didn't, back then. But I believe, if the stories I was always told were true, that she did have a chance to hold me just before I was taken away by my adoptive mother. And she gave me a name.

I had to find her.

I turned my attention back to my maternal tree. Thanks to information I'd gotten from that third cousin I'd met, I had been able, with certainty, to narrow my focus down to one large family. There were six siblings, four boys and two girls, who had immigrated to the US from Belarus as children in 1910, along with their mother and father, who would have been my great-grandparents. The generation that immediately followed the six siblings numbered seventeen in all. I had investigated as many of the seventeen as lined up with what I already knew, i.e. approximate date of birth, gender, and location. There were two sisters who had initially looked like real possibilities. But now, both were looking more and more like probable dead ends. And then I realized something: somehow, I'd neglected to investigate the background of one of the original six, one of the two girls. I set to work to see what I could find out about her. It wasn't long before a marriage record popped up during an Ancestry document search. She had married a man with the surname *Krimsky*.

BINGO.

The whole time, this pivotal information had been sitting there, just waiting to be found with a simple click! I knew in my gut that this was about to be IT. I just had to follow this lead a little bit further. These people would almost certainly have been my maternal grandparents – if they'd had a daughter. A bit more probing and I found that indeed, they had, and while she would have been twenty-three at the time of my birth and not eighteen, as I'd always believed, the difference was negligible. Everything else fit.

I now had the all-important name of the young woman who very likely had given birth to me. I dug a bit deeper. Before long, I found a document listing the name and birthdate of a daughter. My heart nearly stopped. I breathed an expletive in shock. This really WAS it. This other child had been born five years after me, 3,000 miles across the country, and had been fathered by a different man. But her first and middle names were exactly the same as mine at birth, chosen *again* for a second child who would be kept. There was no way that all these things could possibly be a coincidence. I had found my mother at last.

There was abundant proof, and it was irrefutable. Now, all that remained was the dreaded phone call or letter. But I had come too far to give up now. Our mother had died years before, I was sad to learn, but I had a sister, and no doubt she could tell me a lot – if she were willing.

I decided to call instead of write. I was too excited to wait for a letter to travel across the country and maybe get tossed into the trash, or for an answer that could also take quite a while, if it ever came. I'd found the phone number in an internet search and one evening, I dialed.

A man answered, her husband I assumed. I got as far as "Hi, my name is Renée Tone. I have reason to believe that I am closely related to your wife" before he hung up, a very common reaction in this scenario. Undaunted, I immediately called back. Not surprisingly, I got the answering machine this time. I made sure to leave a detailed message, mentioning significant family names, and then I hung up and crossed my fingers.

Several days passed and I heard nothing from her. Then, one evening, the phone rang. It was my sister. Apparently, she'd been trying to reach me for days, but my answering machine had been malfunctioning! No matter. We had finally connected! I told her my story and why I believed that her mother had also been mine. I didn't even have to ask her if she'd be willing to take a DNA test. She suggested it herself, which was a huge relief. I couldn't have been happier, because of course, I already knew what the outcome would be. It was wonderful that she was willing and eager. I wouldn't have to fight to be taken seriously.

I ordered the test for her, and while I waited for the process to unfold, I sent away for my original birth certificate from the state of Florida. Although it is a closed state, an adoptee can get his/her original birth certificate, provided there are letters of permission from the adoptive and birth parents, or their death certificates. I was able to get all four death certificates, my adoptive parents having passed away some years earlier, and eagerly, I filled out the form, got it notarized, enclosed the necessary paperwork, and a check for $15. I made sure, too, to enclose a letter drawing attention to the fact that my mother's surname on my birth certificate would probably be different from the one on her death certificate, because most likely, she would have lied about names and possibly other details.

The third weekend of March, 2018, everything came together in a spectacular way. That Friday, the 23rd, I received a large brown envelope in the mail from Florida. With shaking hands, I opened it and drew out a copy of my original birth certificate, a document I'd waited for my whole adult life. As I suspected, the names had been changed (rather clumsily!) – my mother's maiden name and my father's surname, which was also listed as her married name – as well as their ages, professions, and alleged marital status. Here was the origin of the fabricated surname "Curti" and all the other lies. Fortunately, the clerk who had handled my request for my birth certificate was smart and sensible enough to see past the changes and understand that with these fabrications, my mother had been trying to hide her identity and protect her reputation any way she could. I called my sister, breathless with excitement. If the state of Florida officially recognized this woman as my mother, then surely my sister would as well.

Amazingly, the very next day, her DNA results came back from Ancestry. It was also her birthday. We were a definite half-sibling match, sharing 1,655 centimorgans of DNA. That was the final piece of evidence she needed – what a birthday present! – although it would take a while for all of this momentous news to really sink in and make sense to her.

I know she was in shock for quite some time. It was a lot to absorb all at once. Our mother had taken a huge secret to the grave. No doubt she'd felt terrible grief, guilt, and shame for giving up her flesh and blood, her firstborn. I have subsequently read many books written from the perspectives of adoptees and birth mothers. One in particular, *The Girls Who Went Away* by Ann Fessler, is an illuminating study, drawn from firsthand accounts, of what those girls who were forced to give up their babies went through; this one devastating event affected the rest of their lives, and in many cases, shook their feelings of self-worth to the core. I know now that in some very significant ways, the rest of my mother's life paralleled those accounts of debilitating loss that I read about in Fessler's book. As a mother myself, I can only feel the deepest empathy for the pain she must have experienced, and sadness too, because I will never have the opportunity to look into her eyes, hug her, and tell her I understand and forgive, that I know she didn't have a real choice. Society, religious institutions, and mortified parents joined together to prevent young women from having any real options in such a circumstance. Intense shame and guilt were used as bludgeons. In many cases, young women would give birth and then never be permitted to see their babies at all. They were not told their rights. All they were told was that the whole heartbreaking affair needed to be put behind them, to be forgotten, erased, as if it had never happened at all. Except that it doesn't work that way when the heart is involved. Those mothers never forgot. I am sure my mother never forgot either. And from what I've learned about her from my sister, I don't think she ever forgave herself.

Seven months after that remarkable weekend, my sister came to visit me. We met in Manhattan in the lobby of her hotel. It was an incredible moment, seeing each other for the first time in the flesh. We had a very long hug, and I remember both of us were near to tears. The next several hours were spent just talking over a very long dinner at a restaurant around the corner. We drank really good wine and talked long past finishing our meal, and nobody bothered us to order more food or leave. It was truly one of the most amazing days of my life. I learned so much about our mother's life in the years after I was born: what sort of parent she was, what her interests and talents were, how she lived her life. The more information I learned, the more I hungered to know. Throughout those four hours, both of us were processing a lot. It's quite a momentous thing, discovering a sibling and having to fill in so many blanks, both for oneself and for the sibling who, until relatively recently, had no idea that you even existed.

In subsequent days, we spent time together with both my own family and also with a first cousin of our mother who is now quite elderly. She and our mother had been very close as children, so that experience proved illuminating for my sister as well as for me, since our mother had not been very family oriented once she'd moved across the country and had not stayed in touch with any relatives apart from our grandparents and uncle.

In the three years since that first visit, we've had a second one, just as wonderful, and most recently, I got to meet my niece, who was in Washington, DC, to see a friend and made a special trip up to NYC just to meet her "secret aunt," as she refers to me. My sister and I are in touch by phone and text, and it's been truly lovely, getting to know her. My family and I have since been invited to my niece's upcoming wedding; we've already been to a bridal shower, a wedding, and three baby showers on the paternal side of the family. None of this would ever have been possible without Ancestry and the many doors I have been able to open there. I've gained the knowledge of my roots that I wanted and searched for, and I've also gained some truly wonderful family members, namely a sister, a niece, a nephew, and cousins spanning two generations. My own children have gained an aunt as well as all those cousins, some of whom are close to their own age, several also having children now. How lucky I am, not only to have a warm and close adoptive family, but now to be able to count my newfound relatives as cherished parts of my life.

These days, I am enjoying making further discoveries about potential family members dating back several hundred years. At this point, the endeavor is strictly for fun, as I love research, genealogy, and history, and this sort of fascinating digging satisfies my love of all three.

But I will never forget the singular experience that was my own journey. It was long, sometimes frustrating and confusing, but always intriguing and compelling. My quest for the answers that mattered most to me is now complete. I am happy to share it and to know that it will be passed down as the family continues to grow.

WAYWARD SON
STEPHEN D. EDWARDS

The chainsaw cuts its way into one of the largest trees in our assigned square mile of forest. I stop the cut and look at my son Taylor who holds his hands over his ears. I set the saw back onto the trunk of the tree for another cut and throttle it, showering wood chips and sawdust six feet away.

With the notch cut complete, I idle the saw again and burst out of my silence on the elephant in the forest to ask my son, "Why didn't you bring your ear protection?"

Taylor looks at me with his mouth open staring at me letting me think, *I wonder if he thinks I should know his answer somehow. Then again, he's always been forgetful.*

I turn to the other side of the tree to make the final cut, sending more wood to the forest floor. As the tree cracks at the base and falls to the ground, Taylor yells, "Sorry, Pop!" just audible over the crash. After the noise dies down he continues, "I don't feel productive at the moment and think I should just sit in the truck."

After looking back over the litter of logs below the canopy after three hours on site, I smile at him for a moment until his eyes brighten. Then I say, "Taylor, I've been waiting for you to say something like that since you held your hands over your ears at the first tree this morning. Go to the truck and get the earplugs in the console."

The echoes of his laughter among the trees leave me smiling at his joy of life. I look around to consider the beauty of the forest we harvest this week. As I begin to cut branches from the felled tree I remember just how grateful I am that we decided to apply a conservationist approach to our harvesting methods. Taylor's joy is a good distraction right now.

Taylor returns with his earmuffs on instead of the earplugs. He sees my confused face and says, "I found them peeking out at me from under the passenger seat."

I smile and give him a thumbs up then point him to the top end of the tree saying, "Then you know what to do then."

As the youngster walks down the hill to the other end of the tree, I wonder whether he will ever get it together. Then, I remember how I was a forgetful young man myself. So, I remind myself that just as I grew out of it, he will too.

On our way home I say, "Taylor, we had a rough start, but you did well today. I think tomorrow I will show you everything you need to know about the choice of tree and how to cut it down."

"Thanks, Pop."

The next day the pine needles on the branches gleam with water droplets from an early morning of Pacific coastal rain.

Taylor says, "I've always wondered what that smell is after it rains sometimes."

"It's ozone that is formed from the release of static electricity in the rain clouds when it rains."

Taylor says, "I guess it also means we won't have to worry about a forest fire for a while."

"Yes. That is a comfort I've appreciated for many years in this business. The bonus this morning is that even though it rained, it's not too wet to work. Let's cut down this tree here."

"Pop, why are we choosing this one?" Taylor asks.

"I almost forgot about yesterday's promise. Thanks for reminding me, Son," I reply. "This one is one of the largest trees here. When I checked the area before we started harvesting, I chose the largest and healthiest looking trees. Choosing these trees leaves room for the smaller, younger trees to grow in their place. I also marked them."

Just as I lift the chainsaw to start it up, Taylor asks, "So when do we haul the logs out?"

"I've already arranged for that. I just need to make a phone call the day before we need the truck," I reply. "Now, I'll explain what each of the cuts will do for us."

I point downhill of the tree saying, "We want the tree to fall that way, because there is a space there for it to fall and the fall won't break the lumber." I inspect the trunk of the tree to mark the locations for a notch. I explain, "I want to make a notch and point in the direction I want the tree to land."

As I finish the cuts on the notch and move to the back of the tree to finish felling the tree, I have Taylor's attention as he gives me a thumbs-up. Then, just as I planned, the tree fell where I aimed. Then, I remove my earmuffs and say, "The next one is yours." I walk over to another tree I marked and say, "I'll help you with instructions when you need them, but you do the work."

Taylor says, "Okay." Then, he begins to look downhill for a possible landing area. He points in his selected direction and asks, "Will right there between those two trees work?"

"Yes. It's perfect because there's lots of space between the trees, and there's a good place for it to land on the forest floor," I respond. Little does he know that I picked this tree for him to cut down because it's an easy one. He lines up his cuts and they appear good to go.

He looks at me and asks, "What do you think?"

"It looks like a good setup, Taylor. Now, make sure that when you make the cuts that you cut only as far as you need to make the notch." As I watch him cut the notch, I notice that the cuts are too deep and that the tree is doomed to fall hard and break. Before he's finished making the back-cut, the tree starts to creek like an old ship on the ocean, but it gets louder and louder as the tree falls over. Then, it falls so far left that it hits one of the goal post trees.

Taylor says, "I guess we'll need to take that one down now too. And, is this one only good for pulp now?"

"Son, let's chalk it up to a lesson rather than a mistake," I say with a smile. "Let's cut five more down today and go home."

At home we find my oldest son, Neil cooking dinner at the stove. I ask, "Where is Mom?"

"She's taking a nap," he replies.

"How was work today?" I ask.

"It was awesome, Dad! It's good to feel productive."

I also find a letter in the mail from the University of Chicago for Taylor and hand it to him. I tell him, "Open it. I know that this is the school you want to attend. I've been praying that they accept you."

Taylor opens the letter and reads, "Dear Mr. Taylor Samuelson, Congratulations! With great pleasure, I am writing you to offer you admission to the University of Chicago's Pre-Med School for 2030."

He looks up at me from the watermarked page of the letter with watery eyes and reaches his arms to embrace me which I return with strength. I say, "I'm proud of you, Son."

"Thanks, Pop. I'm gonna make you real proud when I'm done," he declares.

We spend the summer felling 200 or so trees, and Taylor learns so much about the business that I begin to think he really does want to take the logging business over from me. But late in August, Maria and I take Taylor to the Portland International Airport for his flight to Chicago.

After checking him in for the flight, Maria and I both smile at Taylor as I say, "Have a good flight, Son. I will miss you in more ways than one," thinking about the logging work ahead.

"Thank you, Pop. I'm gonna miss you too." Before Taylor releases his hug, he reaches his arm toward Maria and ropes her into the embrace adding, "I'm gonna miss you too, Mom."

"I will miss you too. Call us when you get there," says Maria "This is about your career. Your own adventure." Maria and I stand arm in arm watching as Taylor makes his way into obscurity in the security line.

I continue logging with a new apprentice until the first snowfall and get ready for winter.

On the way home from a logging site, Joe calls me exclaiming, "Guillermo, I didn't know that your son is in Chicago!"

"Yes, Joe. I forgot to share that with you. How did you find out?"

"My niece Andrea told me about him. I don't know if I should tell you about this, but I'm getting a sense that I should somehow. He's been going to many fraternity and sorority parties, drinking all night every night."

I remain calm saying, "Thanks for letting me know. God will bless you for this. Have a great evening."

"Thank you. You too, my friend."

Just before spring break as I look over the season's assigned logging site, my phone rings. It is my dear friend, Joe. He says, "Taylor now has a cocaine habit and is failing all his courses."

"Thanks for letting me know, Joe. But I already know."

Joe asks, "How did you find out?"

"I have sources you don't know about."

He says, "Okay. Have a great day then."

Joe's report breaks my heart, and I thought for a moment that I could call Taylor. But, I know that there's nothing I can tell him. He already knows my desires for him and the right thing to do. Unfortunately, after this call from my dear friend, years pass by as Maria and I think about Taylor without hearing his voice on the phone. I don't know how his schooling has progressed or if he has continued to pursue his dream of becoming a doctor.

One night in the deep of winter when the snows near Wallowa Lake make the mountains appear as though they hang from the sky, my phone rang. Call display said it was from an Illinois number. I answer the phone to hear Taylor's unmistakable voice say, "Father, I've done poorly and dishonored you. I don't expect you to consider me your son. Please, hire me as your assistant. I will do everything you tell me to do."

"Son, it's wonderful to hear your voice! Where are you?"

"I'm at the East St. Louis, Illinois police station," Taylor responds as his voice cracks. "This is my one call. I've been arrested for dealing drugs. I don't want to do this anymore."

"Taylor, don't worry. I'll get you home." I hang up the phone and call my attorney to give him specific instructions. Maria breathes a heavy sigh of relief and says, "My Taylor will be home soon."

"He *will* come home, Maria. I don't mean to change the subject, but have you planned my retirement party?"

She responds, "Yes. Everything is ready for the date you planned."

"Let's make sure we've invited all of our friends and business associates."

On the morning of my planned retirement party, as Maria opens the newspaper she reads the front page headline: OREGON MAN AIDS FBI AND DEA IN MAJOR DRUG BUST.

The article tells of how Taylor played a pivotal role in identifying the drug lords in the gang he became involved in, and how he testified in the trial that resulted in the convictions of those leaders. Thoughts about the article bring a smile to her face as she prepares breakfast for us before our trip to Twin Rocks for the party. She asks, "Is Taylor meeting us there?"

"Yes. He and Mr. Gregoire have already arrived in Portland and are driving there now even though they're tired from the week-long trial in East St. Louis."

"Won't he need a change of clothes?" she asks.

"I've taken care of that already."

Neil, Maria and I drive south along the Oregon coast to Twin Rocks where some friends of mine make preparations for the party in my honor at the hour of my retirement. The parking lot of the hall is sprinkled with SUVs and pickup trucks waiting for the other vehicles to arrive delivering guests to the party.

Mr. Gregoire drives into the lot soon after with our precious cargo from the Portland airport. Taylor looks at me with a furrowed brow, moping with a slow pace toward me.

"Son! It's so good to see you!" I exclaim.

He looks up at me and starts, "Pop, I'm not sure I shou — "

"Of course you should be here, Taylor," I interrupt. "Go inside and talk to John. He has something there for you."

Inside the hall, Taylor takes clothes from John and goes into the bathroom to change. As we enter the main part of the hall, I see the team needs no direction from me regarding the plans for the party as everything is ready to go.

As the time nears, Neil stands beside us as Maria sees Taylor exit the bathroom dressed in my black tails and a bow tie from my wedding day. She turns to me and says, "Guillermo, did you really give the tails to Taylor for this occasion? I thought you were to be the honored guest at this party."

"This will be a complete surprise to everyone!"

Taylor looks up at the beams and wonders at the thought that they could have been made from lumber his dad cut down.

I sidle up beside my son to look up at the beams and confirm, "I cut all this wood down at the foothills of Mount St. Helen before the eruption of 1980."

He turns to me and says, "Wow!"

Looking around the hall I decide the time is right and head to the podium on stage. "Friends and family, thank you all for coming. Make yourselves at home. Lunch will be served at noon, but let me make this small announcement." I look up to see Taylor staring at me — eyes wide. "Today, I am pleased to announce that my son has returned to me after staying away from home for a long time. Some of you may recognize that he wears the same tails I wore on my wedding day." I look up at Taylor to see him looking down at the jacket and back up with a look of surprise. "I will let you all know what the significance of this is after we eat, but I want to welcome you all."

The small crowd applauds. Then I say, "I will pray to get this event started. Lord, we give thanks for this food we are about to receive and ask that it be good nourishment for our bodies. In Jesus name. Amen."

The room becomes loud with the hush of conversations between friends and family present along with the clashing of dishes and cutlery at the sumptuous buffet with lamb, goat, potatoes, carrots and beets along with a garden salad and coleslaw.

After lunch I say to Taylor, "Come with me, Son." I return to the podium with my son in tow and step up to the podium again. "Friends and family, I don't want to take a lot of your time from your dessert, but there is no better time to make this announcement. Many of you already know that I have retired this year from the logging business having had a great career and that may come as no surprise to you. However, this is the moment for which I have asked you all to attend here at this event. My son Taylor will be the one who takes over as CEO of Samuelson Logging Ltd. It was for this announcement that I had Taylor dress in my tails here today." I turn to Taylor and embrace him.

The crowd erupts in shouts and applause across the hall with everyone participating in the celebration of the announcement. As the sounds of joy lessen, Taylor and I make our way back to our table. As I sit down, Neil says, "Dad? I've never strayed from you, still you haven't even given me dinner at home for me and my friends. But, Taylor returns after deserting and dishonoring you and our family, and you throw this lavish feast! Then you make him the CEO of your business?"

"Son, you are with me always, everything I have is yours. Your brother was all but dead and came back alive. We are here to celebrate that he was lost, and now he is found."

WHAT'S IN A NAME?

JASMINE TRITTEN

Can a name produce joy? In my case it did in 1990, the day I married my husband Jim in Monterey, California and took his surname "Tritten." For the rest of my life, I was going to hear the vibrations of that name in my ears, see it written in front of my eyes, and sign it on various pieces of paper. I never met anybody before with such a last name. The lilt of the sound made me happy, but where did the name come from, I wondered? I needed to know.

"Where did your last name Tritten originate?" I asked Jim one day and got a long answer.

"Well, I really don't know for sure. My Dad told me the name was Swiss. But, I thought it originated in a small town in Germany named *Trittenheim* – Tritten home. So, while traveling in Europe, I stopped by the village, went to a hotel in the center and asked if there were any Trittens living in the area. No, they answered and shook their heads. As a last attempt, I walked to the square in the middle of town and yelled "*Ich bin ein Tritten*," which means I am a Tritten, but nobody came."

I chuckled hearing his amusing response, but noticed he tilted his head down and frowned which made me realize he was disappointed over no responses. Because he was busy with work, Jim did not do any further research of his name. Besides, the internet and iPhones did not exist yet. With no ancestry.com, it became difficult to gather facts about families or ancestors.

The following year, we received answers from Jim's sister. She informed us of a Tritt Family newsletter, circulating in various countries. It included research and family history of the Tritten name. We subscribed and discovered ancestors dating back to 1485 in a small village named Lenk of the *Simmental* Valley in Switzerland. To find out more information, we needed to visit the place ourselves.

Two years later a perfect opportunity presented itself. Jim came home from work, his face beamed.

"I am invited to give a lecture at a one-week conference in Switzerland at the Institute of International Studies in Geneva and you can go with me. We can create an exciting trip together."

The moment he mentioned Switzerland, I jumped up and down and found the National Geographic atlas. On the map, I noticed right away the short distance from Geneva to Jim's ancestral town in the German-speaking part of Switzerland. If we took a fast train over the Alps, we might be able to arrive there. Excited about the prospect, we decided to visit Lenk after the conference.

I phoned to book a room in advance. Only one place in Lenk opened in the springtime, the slowest time of the year, between their busy winters and summers.

"Hello, is this Hotel-Pension *Mittaghorn* in Lenk?" I asked.

"Yes, can I help you?" A lady answered in English with a strong German accent.

"We are Mr. & Mrs. Tritten from California in the United States of America. We would like to make a reservation for three nights at your pension," I requested.

"Okay, may I have your information please?"

While I made all the arrangements, we chatted. At the end of the conversation she said,

"Herr Vogel, my husband, will pick you up at the train station in Lenk, when you arrive."

For a moment, I gasped over her generosity. "Thank you so much. Please, tell your husband that Mr. Tritten is very tall with a large moustache and my hair is blonde. I will be wearing a purple hat, so he can find us."

When I put down the receiver I smiled. *All I gave her was my last name. I cannot believe how friendly she is, and she doesn't even know me. This is going to be a great adventure.*

The conference in Geneva ended after one week, and I pulled out the train tickets leading to our destination in Lenk. Before I knew it, I sat bumping shoulders with my husband in the comfort of the spectacular Panoramic Express. With lightness in my chest, I looked in awe through the windows. First, we traveled along beautiful Lake Geneva until we reached Montreux where we changed trains. From there, we zig-zagged through the snow capped mountains of the Alps all along the way. What a sight with icy glaciers imprinted in my mind forever.

After four thrilling hours, the most charming and romantic little village appeared. A valley filled with two-story wooden houses decorated with carvings and window shutters painted in all colors of the rainbow. Smoke billowed from chimneys and dissipated into the thin air. *This is like a fairytale.* A large sign outside read LENK with capital letters.

"We are here!" I said to Jim and stood up from my seat. *I wonder if we will meet anybody with the name of Tritten.*

With our luggage in hand, we stepped down from the train onto the platform and spotted someone waving at us. A small-framed man approached us in a deep brown overcoat, wearing a green felt hat with a feather.

Turning towards Jim I said, "I guess it must be Herr Vogel from Hotel-Pension *Mittaghorn*, ready to drive us there."

"You must be Mr. & Mrs. Tritten. Welcome to Lenk." Herr Vogel had a pleasant voice. He reached out to shake our hands. "Let me carry your suitcases to my car and off we go."

While we rode towards Pension *Mittaghorn* in his small car, he explained that every April, the local people took a break from tourists. During that time of the year between winter and summer seasons, everybody in Lenk stopped working.

"Only two hotels keep their doors open. *Kurhotel Lenkerhof* is one of them. Kurhotel means a hotel with mineral baths and physical therapy," he said. "Do you have ten minutes for a quick stop, before I drive you to Hotel-Pension *Mittaghorn?*"

"Absolutely. We have all the time in the world for the next three days," Jim and I answered simultaneously. *I wonder what he has in mind.*

At *Kurhotel Lenkerhof* he stopped the car and asked us to follow him. *This is peculiar. What is he up to?* We strolled through the old yellow hotel building towards a large formal dining room. He pointed inside and said, "Ten local gentlemen from Lenk are attending their weekly social gathering there." We entered the spacious room and had no idea what would happen next, until Herr Vogel began to introduce us to the people around the long table.

Our mouths fell open when we heard of people in the room with the same last name as us. In America, I had never met so many people with the name Tritten in any gathering, not even family. Herr Vogel introduced us to a banker, an insurance agent, a jeweler, a retired army colonel and more with the last name Tritten. *This is mind-blowing.*

Everyone welcomed us like relatives who had just returned home. We hugged, shook hands, toasted with fine Swiss wine, and ended up consuming a delicious lunch together. After a tasty piece of cheese melted in my mouth, I turned to one of the gentlemen and called attention to my plate, "What kind of cheese is this and from where?"

He got up from his chair, walked over to the window and pointed. "From the farm over there."

Soon, the charming wife of a Helmut Tritten joined us. She warmly extended an invitation.

"We would like to invite you and your husband to a *raclette* fondue dinner tomorrow evening at our chalet."

Jim and I knew this special variety of Swiss cheese people would eat warm. *Sounds delicious.* Everybody smiled. *I wonder why they all seem so happy. Maybe because of the mountain air.*

"Thank you. We accept and anticipate a joyous time with you again," I answered with a full heart.

The ten Swiss minutes turned into three hours of wonderful conversation and celebration. Quickly, we became like one big family. They treated us like royalty because we had the same last name as most people in the room. Or, could it be that all the people of the town were just kind and hospitable? *How can a name have this kind of effect?*

As we left through the foyer, framed abstract paintings filled the walls with cool colors, blue, gray, white and black. Apparently, painted by famous Swiss painter Gottfried Tritten, a brother of Walter Tritten, former owner of the Kreuz Hotel in Lenk. Ever since we got off the train in Lenk, the Tritten name followed us. For being so far away from America, we felt like we were home.

When we drove towards Hotel-Pension *Mittaghorn* outside Lenk in the magical fairy tale country, I glanced at the gorgeous snow-covered mountains rising to the south. They resembled ice cream cones topped with whipped cream.

"Hurrah, we have arrived at our destination," Jim said and leaned over to kiss me as we pulled into a most enchanting place. The gracious Frau Vogel greeted us immediately and led us up the stairs to our room on the second floor. Mesmerized with the view, we lowered ourselves down into the carved wooden chairs on the balcony and took in deep breaths of fresh mountain air. From the distance we heard the faint sounds of cow bells ringing. We learned each bell made a different tone, depending on size.

Early the next morning, we put on our hiking boots and walked for miles to the village of Lenk. Barely did we get into town when Jim said, "Look at that huge sign," and pointed to the lettering over a shop reading *Molkerei Tritten*. "It's a milk and cheese shop. Let's go in."

Drawn to the place like a magnet, we stepped inside the shop. The aroma of aged cheeses filled the room and entered my nostrils. A feast for the eyes with stacks of various kinds of cheeses displayed all around the place. The man behind the counter greeted us.

"*Guten Morgen,*" he said and smiled.

"Good morning! We are Mr. & Mrs. Tritten from California," Jim said.

"Welcome to Lenk. Come on in, my name is Hans." He called his wife to come out to meet us and said to her, "These are Trittens from California."

Shortly thereafter, they invited us into the back of the shop to talk about the Tritten family. We sat down in comfortable chairs and talked for hours. These were people we had never met or heard of before. They offered us a huge amount of food to eat, including various kinds of Swiss cheeses. We talked and talked. *This is like instant family, like we have known them forever.*

Besides good historical information, we received souvenirs decorated with the Tritten name. Never had we heard our unique last name mentioned so many times. Never had we seen our last name written in so many places. All of this because of a name. With tears in my eyes, I thanked them for their hospitality.

The following day, we met in town with their son Christian, a dentist. Interested in doing research on the Tritten family, he gave us a copy of his family tree and showed us a stained-glass coat-of-arms with the name Tritten across. A clover depicted in the middle of a blue shield on a red background. Jim liked the design, so we ordered one from Christian and asked to have it shipped to America. Christian insisted upon driving us miles out of town to St. Stephan Church, the ancestral church of Tritten/Tritt descendants around the world. The church dated back to the 15th Century.

"Look at the bell, it's cast with our name TRITTEN on it in huge letters," I said to Jim as I bounced from foot to foot. *This is unbelievable!* We thanked the young man profusely on the way back to town and exchanged names and addresses for future communication.

After returning to Lenk, Jim and I walked through the cemetery and spotted at least fifteen tombstones with the Tritten name. *Unbelievable.* From local information we discovered around one hundred families of the 2,000 inhabitants in town had the name Tritten.

A couple of hours prior to our departure for the United States, we met Kurt Tritten in the Geneva Airport. Hans from the *Molkerei Tritten* in Lenk had arranged this important meeting with the most prominent researcher of the Tritten family from Simmental Valley, his brother Kurt. He explained if Jim could find out the name of his grandfather's father, he would be able to trace his family based on prior research done in the United States and in Switzerland. He also said no one in Lenk had any idea about *Trittenheim* and they assumed someone from the family must have settled there centuries ago.

Thankful for Kurt Tritten's willingness to share historical knowledge of his family, we flew away from Switzerland with valuable information to research, thanks to Jim's warmhearted kinfolk. Besides wonderful memories of the ancestral home, Lenk, we had newfound relatives and friends all because of our last name. In other words, a name can produce joy.

The stained-glass coat-of -arms with the Tritten name now hangs in the window of our hallway greeting everyone who enters our home, including us. Seeing it always brings joy to our hearts. Our coat-of-arms exists as a reminder of what was once our hidden family – a wonderful family we later discovered in a little village nestled deep in the Swiss Alps.

HERE THE WHOLE TIME
AN ESSAY ABOUT FINDING MY FAMILY AGAIN
AMANDA MONTONI

If I told you twenty years ago that I loved my family, I'd be lying. I just didn't know it yet. You see, my family used to be this plethora of all shapes and sizes. Around the holidays, it used to be this force to be reckoned with. Both sides of the family gathered for birthdays, Christmas, Easter, Thanksgiving, etc. You name it and my house was filled to the brim with full, happy bellies and cousins to play with. From the start, my house was this loving place I never wanted to leave. In addition to my parents and brother, I lived with my Mom's parents and my Uncle. All seven of us were cooped up in this colonial home in Queens, which had wall cabin-like paneling that scared the bejesus out of me. There was a shaggy, brown carpet, and a backyard with an above-ground pool. Sambucca, my first cat, first stepped his paws in that house when I was 5 years old. The kitchen was always in motion. My Grandpa Al always sat on the front stoop smoking cigarettes, and my Uncle blasted country music. It was loud, crowded, and the pantries were filled with junk food my Grandma Barabara always spoiled me and my brother with, going against my Mother's wishes.

As I grew older, the house got less and less crowded, especially around the holidays. Each year for each occasion, my family got smaller and smaller and I didn't know why. It took an unexpected toll on me. My happy little bubble of what reality is was being popped. My parents were hesitant to invite my other set of grandparents to my dance recitals, and my extended family to my Sweet 16. I saw my cousins less and less. I saw my Aunts and Uncles less and less. My Grandparents and Uncle moved out. The four of us (me, my parents and brother) moved to another town after I turned 11, and pretty soon, I was left empty around the holidays and birthdays. At 11 years old, I was already nostalgic for the days in Queens and the magic one feels surrounded by people you love celebrating and laughing. We started to spend the holidays split between family friends. We still kept in touch with our extended family some-what, and after my Grandpa Al passed, my Grandma and Uncle moved into our new home. By the time I became 14 years old, I had watched my family disintegrate.

In my senior year of high school, they moved out, leaving our house in Nassau County feeling eerily empty and for me, broken. The magic of Christmas was lost. The stuffiness of Thanksgiving became a way for me to fill a void. Birthdays always had leftover cake. After eating, we just went right back to our corners of the house, not talking to one another, getting lost in the fantasy of movies and television.

That's when I realized, I considered my friends more like family, and I didn't hate it. These were people who I chose to care for and love, and they chose me too. What a great feeling that is. It lifted me up in ways I had no idea were possible. And at 17, I had just begun to understand the concept of the impact it had on me, emotionally, and psychologically.

Around a year or so later, my parents filled me in on the truth of our extended family dynamic. Let's just say that they had problems, just like everyone else, but amplify that a bit. Don't get me wrong, my immediate family had our problems too, but when I found out about the going ons of everyone else, I was happy to be in a not-so-perfect, but tight-nit loving core.

Let's fast forward to January 2017. That was a bad year for the Montoni clan. 7 days into the new year, my Father's father passed, and suddenly my uncles (some of which I haven't seen in 10+ years), my first cousins (some of which I hadn't even met), and my Nonna (who I hadn't seen since I was 13 years old), were practically living in our home. The house was filled again, but this time for sad and unresolved reasons. I didn't know how to feel. I felt nothing when I heard the news that my Nonno died, and that fact alone was a lot for me to handle since I feel everything very deeply. It was the first time in my life I felt cynical. In reality, I hardly knew my Nonno, so of course I would feel a little detached from the situation. All I remember is that he was the man who pinched my cheeks till they hurt and had an Italian accent so thick, and a voice so deep that when he spoke, it sounded like mumbled gibberish. He also had a mustache like the Monopoly man.

I hardly knew these strangers that shared my blood coming over my house every day, and they didn't know who I was, either. I was twenty-three years old, a young woman, and I swear they still saw me as the tiny little curly-haired dancer who kept quiet when she was supposed to. They didn't know my brother, either. He was a twenty-one year old in his last semester of college, whom they praised for "being a man."

What I did feel, however, was severe empathy for my Father. I could only imagine what he must have felt, having unresolved issues and a complicated past with not only his now-gone father, but his mother and 3 younger brothers. My main concern, and my brother's and Mom's, was him. It was our only intention to be there for him. He needed us, and this was our time to be there for him when he has worked so horrendously hard to be there for us for almost thirty years. You see, my parents are different from the rest of their family. They have a different mind-set, and looking at the big picture, my parents made a better life not only for themselves, but for me and my brother. We got so lucky having them as parents, because they taught us so many lessons of life through compassion, understanding, responsibility, and positivity. They are superhumans in my eyes, and I can never express the amount of gratitude, love, and appreciation I have for them.

2017 was a big coming-of-age year for me and my brother, and a turning point for our family. That year got us, the core-four, so close that I now have a different sense of what a family is. All four of us went through a traumatic experience, forcing us to be there for each other like never before. It was the first time I had the experience of taking care of my parents. Whether it was doing certain things for them around the house, running errands, or being there for them emotionally, I had to step up in ways I could to make the situation a little less taxing on them. My Dad has always taken care of his family. His past reflects that, and after years of silence from them, he was back taking care of them.

My Nonna lived with us for 6 months after my Nonno passed. My Mother took care of her every day, even though she was going through a rough time taking care of herself. It was an adjustment for all of us, except my brother who attended college out of state. He would come home and hear me vent about these sudden now-regular Sunday dinners with my Uncles sitting at the table. I would vent about how my Nonna was giving me advice when I was already grown and could navigate through Manhattan by myself, seeing as how in my college days, I commuted every day to school by myself. I had my own life, and there were family members showing up telling me what to do as if I was still a naive, young, teenage girl. I know that they were "looking out for me" but my parents raised me to be safe, responsible, and most importantly, independent. I could take care of myself. Thank you, Mom and Dad.

My Dad became quieter than he used to. He stopped talking at the dinner table. We would look at him, having not touched his food, listening to his brothers who popped back into his life, pondering. Thinking. Feeling. My Mom would do the same thing. I looked at my family from an outside perspective, since I was detached from them a lot more than my parents were, and all I wanted to do was help, but in some cases, there was nothing I could do but let the time pass. For 6 months I was frustrated, angry, and sad because I couldn't do anything significant to help. It was the most angry I have ever been in my life, and it started to affect my work. I was irritable teaching dance classes. I was frustrated in rehearsals for musicals I was chore-ographing. I needed to get out, so what did I do? I tried to surround myself with friends. Those friends, you know who you are, probably don't even know how much you helped me during that time. I hated myself and my life at the time, but you loved me anyway. Thank you.

After 2017, my perspective on what family is has changed. My perspective on who my parents were changed. For the first time, I saw them as actual people who feel things, who problem solve, who pick their stand-up moments carefully. I saw 2 people who fought their past and created a future, only to have the past creep up on them, and then persevere. I saw 2 people with hearts so big and full of giving that they still wanted to help the people they've had complicated relationships with, and that is something truly remarkable in this world. If any one of us in this world is lucky enough, we might come across maybe one of those people in our lifetime, and sitting right in front of me were 2 of them. They are the end-all be-all of role models, and left me with this lesson: Take whatever curveball Life throws at you with grace and patience, and you can hit any home run you want.

Do I still want to have a big tight-nit extended family in the future? Of course I do. I want the whole shabang: a husband, kids, nieces and nephews, cousins, aunts, uncles, you name it. I will treasure those first 10 years of my life in the Queens colonial until the day I die. But maybe, just maybe, the picture will be painted a little different. It will have the colors of family friends, much like my teen years were painted. Maybe those friends have kids of their own and their kids play with my kids. Hey, I can dream, can't I? To this day, I still consider my friends my family. I have a handful of best friends that I would gladly "take a bullet for," so to speak. They chose me, and I chose them. And choosing the people you love is so much more powerful than being forced to love someone just because you share the same DNA or blood. Blood is thicker than water, yes, but not *all* blood is thicker than *all* water, metaphorically speaking.

Now, at 28 years old, I live with my brother. It was definitely an adjustment. I'm not going to sugar coat that. But, given our past, we have come a really long way. He used to drive me completely insane, and I'm not just talking about "pushing buttons" here. We used to have intense arguments and I used to avoid him. He used to knock on my bedroom door as a kid, and I would deny him access or kick him out. I was really quite mean to him. I do have a mean streak. You do not want to piss me off. Words are powerful things, and they can be sharply harsh. In retrospect, I realized I treated him the way I did because I didn't understand him. I realized I was acting quite possibly the way my parent's families did and didn't give him the compassion and understanding that my parents gave us. I was doing the exact opposite of what my parents made sure was different about their parenting styles from their parents. That made my heart so heavy, it affected how I interacted with people. I needed to make a change.

I found out a couple of years ago that my parents decided not to tell me certain things about my brother while we were growing up. Was I upset because maybe I would have treated him with more grace back then? Absolutely. But they were right: I didn't need to know what was going on back then. It was not my concern. My parents wanted me to continue to go through my coming-of-age years at my own pace in my own way, and telling me information that was going to stunt that growth for me in any way would destroy their spirits.

I have never felt closer to my brother than I have now. It took being roommates as adults (and intense, tearful conversations) to actually see and understand the other. Through that, we have found that we are very similar in personality, and that's not just because we are both Cancer signs. We have common interests. We think the same way about some things. We actually enjoy having conversations now. I don't know if he knows this, but he is the person I root for the most. He is a miraculous human being and I hope with all of my heart that he finds his way to make this world his. I have never had someone push me so much in my entire life, and for that I'm grateful. I see the amazement that he is, even when he is going through something, or we have blow-ups that end in screams and tears (I'm talking soap opera level here). My whole family timeline has led me to him. This essay has led me to him. He has been here the whole time working through issues and persevering through what may feel like endless obstacles, just like my parents. All the while, he was always trying to connect with me. I can't even express how sorry I am that it took me so long to realize that. It breaks my heart into pieces, and my eyes are swelling just writing this. He has become my life-long best friend. The only kind of best friend that can be both blood *and* water. For me and my family's history, that is the rarest of rarities to come by.

So, yes. If I told you twenty years ago that I loved my family, I'd be lying. I just didn't know it yet. I didn't know what *family* meant to me. Now, through the ups and downs of life, I have truly found my family, and you know what, I wouldn't have had it done any other way.

ABOUT THE AUTHORS

DON ECKERLE

I was born in Queens, last of 7 children.

I do genealogy as a hobby and I am the database administrator for the German Genealogy Group. We had indexed over 22 million records and have made them available to anyone, free, on our website Germangenealogygroup.org

STEPHEN D. EDWARDS

Stephen D. Edwards regularly contributes to AllAboutChrist.net authored "The Branch and the Vine" a memoir of long-term depression and hope. He also writes novels and short stories with Christian themes. Edwards' most recent work has been published in Agape Review", "Faith on Every Corner", "Calla Press" and "OpenDoor Poetry".

JOAN FOOR

Joan Foor MN, RN a graduate from UCLA worked in the field of nursing for over 40 years. Part of her career included enlisting in the U.S. Army during Viet Nam. She is proud to have enlisted in the WAC Corps and continued to serve in The U.S. Army Reserve Nurse Corps for 26 more years. She retired as Lieutenant Colonel. Joan has written and published five books and loves to travel with her terrier dog in her Rialta R.V.

CHRISTINA HOAG

Christina Hoag is the author of novels Law of the Jungle (Better than Starbucks Press), Girl on the Brink and Skin of Tattoos (both from Onward Press). Her short stories and essays have appeared in literary reviews including Lunch Ticket, Toasted Cheese and Shooter, and have won several awards. For more information: https://christina hoag.com.

DIANE KANE

Author Diane Kane dabbles in all genres and explores every aspect of writing and publishing. She measures her success by the friends she has made along the way. Her short stories and poetry have appeared in numerous Red Penguin publications. Kane is one of the founding members of Quabbin Quill's non-profit writers' group. She is the publisher and co-author of Flash in the Can Number One and Number Two, short stories to read wherever you go. Kane writes public interest articles for Uniquely Quabbin Magazine and newspapers. She published her first children's book, Don Gateau the Three-Legged Cat of Seborga, in 2020, in English, Spanish, French and Italian. The sequel will be published in 2022. Her second children's book, Brayden the Brave, was published in April 2021. She is currently working on a coming of age novel, I Never Called Him Pa.

MICHAEL P. KUSEN

Michael P. Kusen has written and illustrated several poetry chap books as well as instructional chess books – and several of his essays and short stories have been published in anthologies. In addition, he does poetry animations and assemblage art – and occasional presentations on poetry, chess, and memoir writing: mqsen@aol.com.

DAVID LANGE

David Lange was born and grew up on Long Island, New York. A graduate of the United States Air Force Academy, he served for 30 years as an Active Duty officer in the United States Air Force before retiring in 2018. Colonel Lange is a decorated combat veteran and flew numerous combat, combat support, and humanitarian relief missions during his career. He was awarded the prestigious Institute of Navigation Superior Achievement Award in recognition of his life-long accomplishments as a practicing navigator. David loves sharing stories of hope and inspiration. He has numerous short stories, essays, and poems published within various anthologies and his memoir, "Quest: My Journey Through La Mancha," was published in 2020.

AMANDA MONTONI

Amanda Montoni comes from a loud Italian-American family, which explains her loud voice and laugh you can hear from miles away. That voice is put to use, as she is an actress, singer, dance and theater teacher. She is also an award winning Director/Choreographer for the stage and is a co-founder of Royal Star Theatre. She has multiple publications under her belt as a writer. She has published plays, monologues, short stories, and poems in various anthologies with The Red Penguin Collection. One of her plays has been turned into a podcast thanks to Random Thursdays Radio Theatre. She has written two poetry collections that are very near and dear to her heart: Trains, New York, and the Love (or lack thereof) That Goes Along With Them, and Thoughts While Singing. She has lots of projects up her sleeve, and loves the overwhelmingly busy life she has. www.amandamontoni.com @a.montoni.poetry

H. NEWNAM

H. Newnam has had several personal essays published. She is passionate about writing and helping others, and believes her best writing is done with the intention of helping. Her writing is an expression of compassion aimed at influencing people to be brave enough to let go and open up space to let compassion flow in.

WILLIAM JOHN ROSTRON

The author recently published A Flamingo Under the Carousel, a collection of thirty short works that he labels as "fiction, non-fiction, and almost fiction." Previously, he published three novels. Steeped in the late 20th and early 21st centuries' music and culture, these three works (Band in the Wind, Sound of Redemption, and Brotherhood of Forever) have received critical acclaim from Writers Digest, the Online Book Club Review, and many other reviewers. These books have found readership on four continents (North America, Europe, Australia, and Asia).

In the past, he has published over two dozen non-fiction articles in newspapers and magazines. These writings included four full-page op-eds in New York Newsday. He was also presented an award by Nelson DeMille for his historical fiction short story, "The Last Artifact." Recently, his short pieces have been published in a dozen Red Penguin anthologies.

Four of his short pieces were accepted into the Visible Ink anthologies in 2018, 2019, 2020, and 2022. Each year, a dozen works are chosen for reading and presentation on stage in New York City. In 2018, "Pretty Flamingo" was given this honor. As an encore, "In the Garden of Eden" was performed in 2019. In 2020, his short work "Ava's Bubble" was read by Tony and Emmy nominee Victor Garber on a nationally televised streaming show. In 2022, "Fool on the Hill" was performed. All of these are available for viewing on www.williamjohnrostron.com.

Born and raised in Queens, NY, William John Rostron now splits his time between his home on Long Island and traveling the country in his Tiffin motorhome. When not writing, he is busy completing a bucket list of travel adventures. In the past 17 years, he and his wife Marilyn have traveled 130,000 miles. These journeys have taken them to the 48 contiguous states, 133 national parks, all 30 major league baseball stadiums, 154 cities and towns, two Canadian provinces, and a variety of unusual experiences and locations. Many of these locations have served as backgrounds for his books.

In his previous career, the author instructed students from the ages of 9 to 90. In his life, he taught elementary school, middle school, high school, college, adult education, and teacher training. He holds degrees from Queens College, Stony Brook University, and Long Island University.

He presently working on a novel, Lost in the Wind, the fourth book in his Band in the Wind series.

JANET MAIKA'I RUDOLPH

I am a wife, lover, mother, grandmother, seeker, finder, earth-breather, water-swimmer, there is no end to my descriptions. I have traveled to many sacred places in the world to soak up knowledge and experience culture. Along the way I have earned two shamanic initiations and written a few books including When Moses Was a Shaman and When Eve Was a Goddess. I both write and take photos wherever and whenever I can. I do both in order to express, heal, inform, challenge, startle and to expand love. You can find my work at /mysticpagan.com/

RENÉE TONE

Renée Tone is a college professor, museum educator, and writer. Married with two grown children and two young grandchildren, she is an avid gardener and lover of mythology, folklore, fairy tales, history, and animals, cats in particular.

JASMINE TRITTEN

Jasmine Tritten is an award-winning author born in Denmark. In 1964 she immigrated to the U.S.A. During the last five years, she has written numerous short stories published in various anthologies. Her memoir "The Journey of an Adventuresome Dane", published in 2015, won an award. A children's story, "Kato's Grand Adventure," published in 2018, she wrote with her husband and it won five awards. During the pandemic in 2020, Jasmine wrote and self-published a travel book "On the Nile with a Dancing Dane" that won three awards in 2021. Jasmine resides in enchanting Corrales, New Mexico with her husband and four cats.

JANET METZ WALTER

Janet Metz Walter grew up in Queens NY. She realized very early in life that she wanted to write, and throughout her careers in various social service agencies she wrote local newsletters and professional articles.

She also wrote and produced shows in camps and community theater productions.

She has been a travel agent, world traveler and teacher in Adult Continuing Ed in several schools, and has taught classes in the game of Mah Jongg for 18 years.

In 2009 she joined her husband in his fine jewelry business, Gold Fire Diamonds as Vice President in charge of the website and marketing. She realized her lifelong dream when she wrote her book "The 2 Carrot Ring and Other Fascinating Jewelry Stories," a collection of people's personal stories about their pieces of jewelry. She also is available for interactive group programs about the book.

Janet has also contributed to the Red Penguin anthologies "Realiteen:Reflections on Growing Up" and "Feeding The Flock:Recipes From the Red Penguin Family.

She is happy to be included in the "Finding Family" anthology.

Connect with Janet Metz Walter

Facebook-Janet Metz Walter

Amazon.com/author/janetmetzwalter

Goodreads author Janet Metz Walter

janetwalter.bsl@gmail.com

www.goldfirediamonds.com

ALSO FROM THE RED PENGUIN COLLECTION

POETRY

Words for the Earth – A Poetry Project

'Tis The Seasons – Poems to Lift Your Holiday Spirits

the flower shop on the corner – A Spring Poetry Anthology

the ocean waves – A Summer Poetry Anthology

the leaves fall – An Autumnal Poetry Anthology

FICTION

What Lies Beyond – Sci-Fi Stories of the Future

I Can't Find My Flashlight – Contemporary Campfire Stories

A Heart Full of Love – A Collection of Romantic Short Stories

Behind Closed Doors – A Mystery Anthology

Once Upon A Time... – A Fairy Tale Anthology

Ernest Lived ...and other Historical Fiction Short Stories

Until Dawn – A Supernatural Anthology

Treat-or-Trick – Halloween Horror Stories

Pets On the Prowl – An Animal Mystery Anthology

My Robot & Me – A Not-So Fiction Anthology

THE STAND OUT SERIES

Stand Out – The Best of The Red Penguin Collection, Vol. 1

Stand Out – The Best of The Red Penguin Collection, Vol. 2

* 9 7 8 1 6 3 7 7 7 3 6 6 6 *